Card Game Roundup

Play your Way to Math Success

by Trudy Bortz
and Josh Rappaport

Card Game Roundup

Play your Way to Math Success

Published by:
Singing Turtle Press
#770, 3530 Zafarano Drive #6
Santa Fe, NM 87507

Tel: 1/505-438-3418
Fax: 1/505-438-7742
www.SingingTurtle.com
E-mail: kyle@SingingTurtle.com

ISBN: 0-9659113-0-6

The publisher expresses appreciation to Clare Schoolmaster, Jennifer Kadlubek, and Toni Burger, who tested many of these games in their classrooms and provided invaluable feedback. The publisher also thanks Kathy, Ari and Ella Rappaport, who helped develop these games and offered many suggestions. Thanks, too, to Suzanna Bortz, for feedback and ideas.

— Attention Teachers / Administrators —
For information on volume discounts to schools, visit us at: SingingTurtle.com
Or call us at the phone number above.

Contents

Howdy, Educators!

Ever yearn to find games that not only teach vital math skills, but engage children so much that they beg you to play them?

Consider yourself fortunate. You just found a book that does just that.

In this book, we've rounded up 17 delightful games, quite unlike those in other supplemental math books. In most math supplements, the "games" simply reinforce concepts through drill and practice.

In Card Game Roundup, we present games that actually teach the concepts, and which are loads of fun, to boot. That means that you, the educator, can use these games to actually teach, not just review or practice.

In the Mysterious Bandits game, for example, children don't just work two-digit addition / subtraction problems; they learn the intricacies of such problems. Read through our friendly Campfire Chat questions following the rules. You'll see that even as children seek the identity of those dastardly, masked bandits, they discover connections between addition and subtraction, gaining insights that help them work such problems with ease and understanding.

How about functions? When children play Bucking Bronco, they not only learn what functions are, they actually create their own functions, and figure out the rules behind other children's functions And they'd best be careful. For if not, they get bucked off the bronco!

Then there's geometry. Area and perimeter, to be exact. In Cows in the Pen, children not only learn what area and perimeter are, they also get challenged to maximize area given a fixed perimeter. All in the name of making a pen to hold the most cows.

These are examples from just three games in this collection. Other games teach the concepts of: attributes and sets, Venn diagrams, rules for adding and subtracting odd and even numbers, sequences and patterns, bar graphs and scatter-plots, measurement, process of elimination, even combining positive and negative integers! In short, the very kinds of math skills and concepts that children need today, now that the National Council of Teachers of Mathematics has broadened the notion of a good elementary school math education.

Here's something else. Every game comes with its very own "Storyline." That's a tall tale that engages children and makes the game more fun to play. Studies have shown that young children learn better when their imaginations are engaged, and that's just what these storylines do.

The games are flexible, too. Depending on the chldren you're working with, you can choose whether children play cooperatively or competitively. Most games have both kinds of versions.

The games may be played in large groups, small groups, or individually. It often helps to teach the games to a large group using overhead projector cards and making transparencies of the necessary gameboards. Then let children play the games in small groups.

We hope you enjoy using these card games. And we wish you happy trails!

How to Use the Ikons

Card Game Roundup uses ikons to guide you through the games. Here's a view of the ikons and a description of how they can help you.

STORYLINE, in the upper-left corner of each game's opening page, provides a story that grounds the game in a Wild West theme.

We suggest that the Educator read the **STORYLINE** aloud to children, for the more they connect with the story, the more engaged they will be in playing the game.

CONCEPT CORRAL, located just below **STORYLINE,** details the NCTM standards involved in each game: Number & Operation, Geometry, Problem Solving, Connections, etc. Each subsection of the **CORRAL** offers details on how the game meets the standard.

Use **CONCEPT CORRAL** to document how using the book helps you meet the math standards and competencies in your area.

Note that a chart on p.96 conveniently displays the NCTM standards involved in each of the 17 games.

CAMPFIRE CHAT

CAMPFIRE CHAT offers follow-up questions and activities that help you bring out the rich mathematical content in the games. For educator's convenience, answers are provided for the Campfire Chat questions.

CAMPFIRE CHAT questions may be used for math journal entries. You will find an asterisk (*) by those questions that make particularly good journal entries. Since every game poses Campfire Chat questions, every game addresses NCTM's Communication standard.

TIPS AND POINTERS

TIPS and **POINTERS,** in the black box after **CAMPFIRE CHAT,** offers time-tested advice for each game.

Read through the **TIPS** and **POINTERS** before playing to develop strategies that make optimal use of each game.

ROUNDUP

ROUNDUP does just what you'd expect ... tells you the supplies to rustle up before children can play.

Most supplies are readily at hand, and the book provides the reproducible worksheets and gamesheets you need.

ROUNDUP is found in the margin on the right-hand page of every game spread.

There's a wild bull at this year's rodeo called "Nine-Second" Ned, so named because no cow rustler has ever ridden him for 10 seconds or more (though a few have held on for an amazing nine seconds). Young rodeo stars try to stay on Ned for the maximum of nine seconds, but not a second longer. If they do this enough times, they may just win the Rodeo Trophy.

CONCEPT CORRAL

NUMBER & OPERATION

➤ Count to nine and beyond.

➤ Add a string of whole numbers.

DATA ANALYSIS

➤ Figure out whether or not drawing a card might push a card total beyond nine.

PROBABILITY

➤ Study odds of getting a card that would be in a child's favor.

REASONING

➤ Determine how safe it is to take another card.

CONNECTIONS

➤ Discover links between addition and probability.

6

"Nine-Second" Ned

GAME A Cooperative

GOAL: Aspiring rodeo stars work together to collect enough tokens to win the Rodeo Trophy.

 # Players: 1, 2, 3, or 4.

1 Children shuffle deck and place it face down. They put 10 to 20 tokens in a bowl or container called "the pot." Children take four tokens from the pot and place these tokens on the table. Then children turn over the two cards on top of the deck.

2 Children add the two cards, and the sum represents the number of seconds they have stayed on Ned so far. e.g. If cards are 2 and 4, it means they have stayed on Ned for 6 seconds. Children discuss whether or not to take another card.

3 Consequences of card draws: a) If children draw a card that makes their sum 8 or less, they take one token from the pot as a reward, since they have stayed on the wild bull. **b)** If they draw a card that makes their sum 9, they take two tokens from the pot, since they stayed on Ned for maximum possible time. **c)** But if card drawn makes sum 10 or more, Ned knocks them off, and they must return two of their tokens to the pot. (See p.8 for visual explanation.)

4 Children may draw as many cards as they wish or dare on any turn. Also, children don't have to take a card on any turn. But in some cases, they would lose out by not taking a card. e.g. If first two cards have a sum of 3, there's no way to get knocked off by taking a card, since highest card they can get is 4, and 3 + 4 is only 7.

5 Children try to win as many tokens as educator specifies it takes to win Rodeo Star Trophy, which can be copied off the master on p.65. It's fun to start with a goal of 10 tokens, and gradually increase goal number as children become more comfortable with the game.

6 If children run out of tokens, they lose that rodeo match, but start another.

GAME B Competitive

GOAL: Each rodeo hopeful tries to collect the most tokens, or to be the only player with tokens left after all other players have run out. Whoever does so wins the Rodeo Trophy.

 # Players: 2, 3, or 4.

1 Shuffle and place deck face down. Put 10 tokens in the pot for every child playing. Each player takes four tokens from the pot. Child who is dealer gives each player two cards face up.

2 Player to right of dealer checks sum of his two cards. Player tells dealer whether or not he wants another card (he may pass, if he wishes). If he takes a card that makes his cards sum to eight or less, player takes one token from pot. If it makes his cards sum to nine, player takes two tokens from pot. But if it makes his cards sum to 10 or more, player must return two of his tokens to pot. Player may draw as many cards as he wants or dares to take. If a player runs out of tokens, he is out for the rest of that game.

3 Next player takes the same kind of turn as first player.

4 Two ways to win: **a)** be first player to collect 10 tokens, or **b)** become only player with tokens left after all other players have lost their tokens. Either way, winner gets Rodeo Trophy.

1 How did you decide whether or not to take another card? **A: Answers will vary, but children generally realize that it's safer to take a card if they have a lower sum, and riskier to take a card if they have a higher sum.**

2 Did you ever know that it was completely safe to take another card? If so, how did you know? **A: Children should eventually realize that any time their sum is 5 or less, they stand no risk in taking a card. This is because the highest card they can get is a 4, and 5 + 4 = 9, and therefore even with a 4, they take no risk of getting thrown off of Ned.**

3 Did you ever decide it was too risky to take another card? If so, how did you decide? **A: Children eventually realize that the decision should be based on two factors. One: the risk that a card drawn will knock them off Ned. Two: their standing in the game vis-a-vis the other players. That is, even if taking a card may be risky, it could be worth the risk if another player is likely to win on his next turn.**

4 Did you ever feel so motivated to get a 9 that, even though you were close to 9, you drew a card? Did your risk pay off? **A: Answers will vary.**

5 Did your group ever get into an argument over whether or not to take another card? If so, how did you resolve the argument? **A: Answers will vary, but the ideas expressed will reveal children's understanding — or lack of understanding — of the addition and probability aspects of the game.**

FOR EACH CHILD OR GROUP OF CHILDREN:

➺ Deck with just the Aces, 2s, 3s, and 4s. Add Jokers if you want children to see effect of adding 0.

➺ Small bowl or container to put tokens in. This bowl is referred to as "the pot."

➺ Game A: 10 to 20 tokens.

➺ Game B: 10 tokens for each child playing (e.g. 30 tokens for three players).

➺ OPTIONAL: Rodeo Star Trophies copied off master on p.65, to be used as fun rewards.

6 Can you express the odds of getting a safe card in standard probability terms, as in "My odds of getting a safe card are 3 out of 4"? **A: With just a bit of practice, children can learn to express their odds of getting a safe card this way. Example: If they have a sum of 6, THREE of the FOUR possible cards (Ace, 2, and 3) will be safe, so they can, say, "My odds of getting a safe card are 3 out of 4."**

TIPS AND POINTERS

1 It's best to play cooperative game first, so all get comfortable with rules.

2 In cooperative game, encourage children to confer when deciding whether or not to draw another card. Also encourage them to remember what they talk about during conferences, so they can share their ideas during the Campfire Chat.

3 Consider using cards from two or more decks so children play more and shuffle less.

4 To emphasize games's probability aspects, ask children questions as they play. Helpful questions include: **a)** Given the sum you have, are there any cards that would be safe to get? **b)** Are there any cards that could knock you off of Ned? **c)** Of the four kinds of cards in the deck (Aces, 2s, 3s and 4s), how many would be safe to get? How many would knock you off the bull? **d)** Given this breakdown of safe to unsafe cards, do you think it's safe or risky to draw a card? And why?

5 You might suggest that children use a special layout to arrange the tokens they collect. Example: Arrange tokens in rows of 2 to learn to count by 2s; in rows of 5 to learn to count by 5s.

"Nine-Second" Ned Overview

Sum of 8 or less ...
take 1 token.

Sum of 9 ...
take 2 tokens!

Sum of 10 or more ...
return 2 tokens!
Ouch!

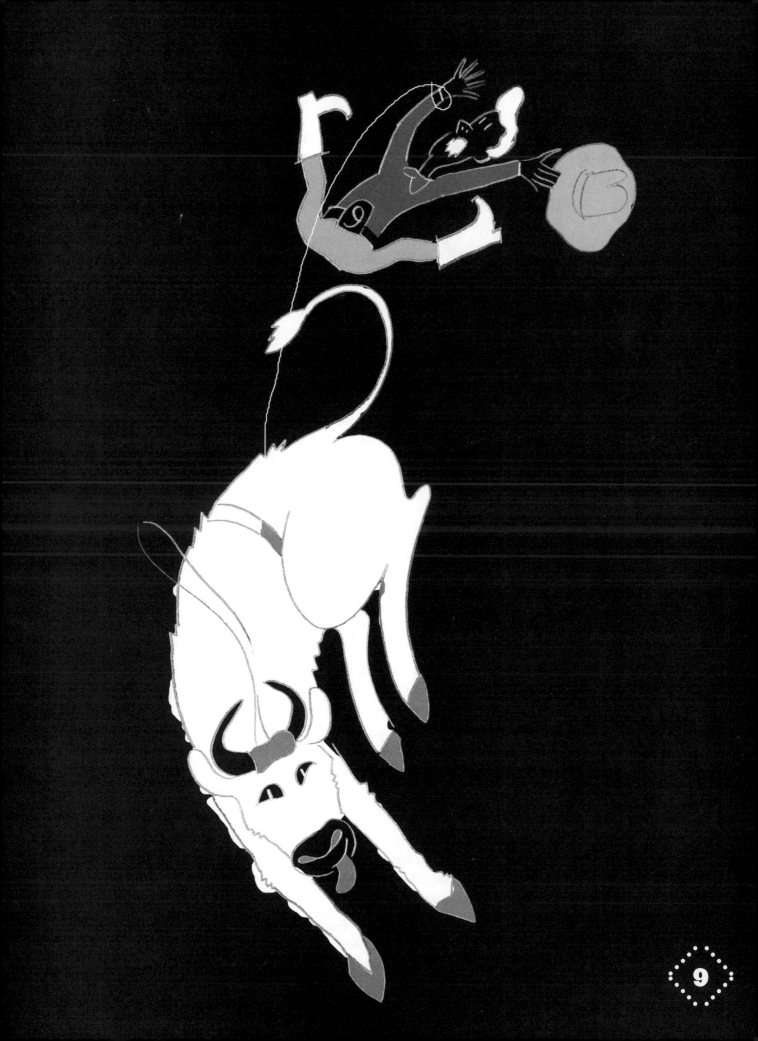

Preparing to compete in the upcoming rodeo, young cowhands practice their skill at hitting a target. To test their skill, they toss different objects into a basket from a variety of distances, and chart their rates of success.

CONCEPT CORRAL

MEASUREMENT
➡ Compare lengths of distances using a nonstandard unit (a cut-out paper horseshoe).

DATA ANALYSIS & PROBABILITY
➡ Discover patterns in data, and analyze how throwing from various distances affects one's rate of success in hitting a target.

REASONING
➡ Develop hypotheses to account for the data.

CONNECTIONS
➡ Find connections between measurement and data analysis.

REPRESENTATION
➡ Record hits and misses on a chart. Then use that data to fill in a bar graph and scatterplot.

10

Annie Oakley

GAME A Cooperative

GOAL: To throw a variety of objects into a basket from a distance determined by a chance draw of a card. Next, to record the result of each throw. Then to represent the data first on a bar graph, then on a scatterplot. Finally, to look for patterns in the data.

 # Players: 1, 2, 3, or 4.

1 Each team chooses an object to throw (see Roundup). It's best if every team uses a different object.

2 Team members number their 10 horseshoes (see Roundup) from 1 to 10 in space provided on left arm of Horseshoe. Children place Horseshoe #1 in front of the wastepaper basket. Then they place the remaining nine horseshoes behind the first horseshoe, sequentially, in a straight line stretching away from the wastepaper backet.

3 Children shuffle deck and place it face down. On each turn, one child in the team draws top card. Number on card tells child how many horseshoes away from wastepaper basket to stand.

4 Child who drew card takes object to be thrown and stands behind and to the side of the horseshoe corresponding to number he drew.

5 Child throws object, trying to get it into the wastepaper basket. If shot goes in, child marks appropriate face on Annie Oakley Data Sheet with smile; if he misses, he marks face on Data Sheet with a frown.

6 Game continues until children draw all 40 cards and make 40 tosses. (If you prefer quicker game, remove a suit or two and use 30 or 20 cards and throws. But don't use 10; not enough data for analysis!)

7 After children record throws on Data Sheet, they fill out Annie Oakley Bar Graph by coloring up to correct number for each distance. i.e. If they made two shots from a distance of 4, they color the bar up to 2 at the 4 distance. Make sure children understand that if they get no hits at a certain distance, the bar for that distance remains uncolored.

8 After children fill out Bar Graph, they fill out the Annie Oakley Scatterplot by marking the number of hits at each distance and drawing lines connecting the dots. NOTE: Children familiar with scatterplots may skip the bar graph stage.

Follow-Up Activity: Educator holds up one group's bar graph or scatterplot and ask a child from another group if he can read and interpret the data. Children from group whose data is used give feedback as to whether or not child interprets data correctly.

1 Looking at your data sheet, bar graph and scatterplot, what do you notice about your group's success in hitting the target as you stood farther from it? **A: Children should see that they hit target less frequently the farther away from it they stand.**

2 If you see a pattern, how does it show up on the Data Sheet? On the Bar Graph? On the Scatterplot? **A: Data Sheet shows fewer hits at the top, more hits at the bottom. Bar Graph's bars and Scatterplot's lines descend in an overall way from left to right.**

*3 Which was easiest to throw accurately? Which object was hardest? And why? **A: Answers will vary, but often easy-to-grasp and fairly heavy objects, like a bean bag, will produce the greatest results. Children usually see that objects that are relatively undisturbed by air (like bean bags or tennis balls) can be thrown more easily than those that are affected by air (like paper airplanes and crumpled up pieces of paper).**

TIPS AND POINTERS

1 You will need to photocopy and cut out 10 horseshoes per group. Laminating horseshoes ensures they'll last for years. Or you can use another manipulative measuring tool in your classroom such as blocks, rulers, etc. But make sure any manipulative used is at least 10" long. Otherwise it's so easy for children to make shots that they won't get enough misses to create a broad data spread.

2 Show children how to line up horseshoes end-to-end, discussing what happens to measurement's accuracy if children line horseshoes up carelessly.

3 Show children how to record on Data Sheet, Bar Graph and Scatterplot.

4 INTERESTING USE OF SCATTERPLOTS: Copy Scatterplot master onto several transparencies. Give each group one to fill out, and have each group mark theirs up with a different color dry-erase marker. Then put all scatterplots together on an overhead projector. That way, children can compare the various rates of success by seeing how one color compares with another.

5 You can alter game to make it more or less active / noisy depending on your tolerance. If game gets too loud or noisy, have children use smaller horseshoes(such as those on p.87) and smaller target (a can or some other small container), and let them play game on a table.

6 If children have trouble throwing ball into bucket, you may have them roll it to hit bucket.

ROUNDUP

FOR EACH TEAM OR GROUP:

➤ **One deck of the 40 numbered cards (Ace through 10), but no picture cards or Jokers.**

➤ **One Annie Oakley Data Sheet on from p.13, one Annie Oakley Bar Graph from p.14, one Annie Oakley Scatterplot from p.15, and 10 horseshoes copied off the master on p.12.**

➤ **One empty wastebasket or bucket.**

➤ **A variety of different objects that children can throw into the basket. Some good ones are: beanbag, crumpled-up piece of paper, paper airplane, superball, tennis ball.**

11

Annie Oakley Horseshoe Master

Horseshoe #
_____

Annie Oakley Data Sheet

Mark hits by drawing a smile on the face.
Mark misses by drawing a frown on the face.

Card Drawn	Throw #1	Throw #2	Throw #3	Throw #4	Total # Hits
10					
9					
8					
7					
6					
5					
4					
3					
2					
1					

Annie Oakley Bar Graph

Color space between bars to show number of hits at each distance.

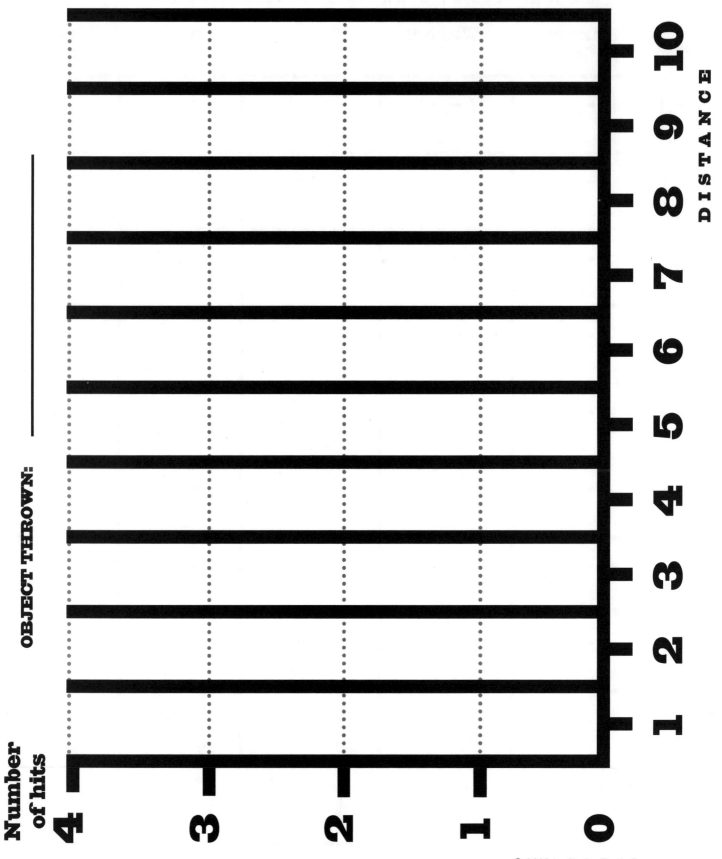

OBJECT THROWN:

Number of hits

4 3 2 1 0

1 2 3 4 5 6 7 8 9 10

DISTANCE

Annie Oakley Scatterplot

Shade in the small circles to indicate number of hits at each distance.
Then draw straight lines connecting the circles to create your scatterplot.

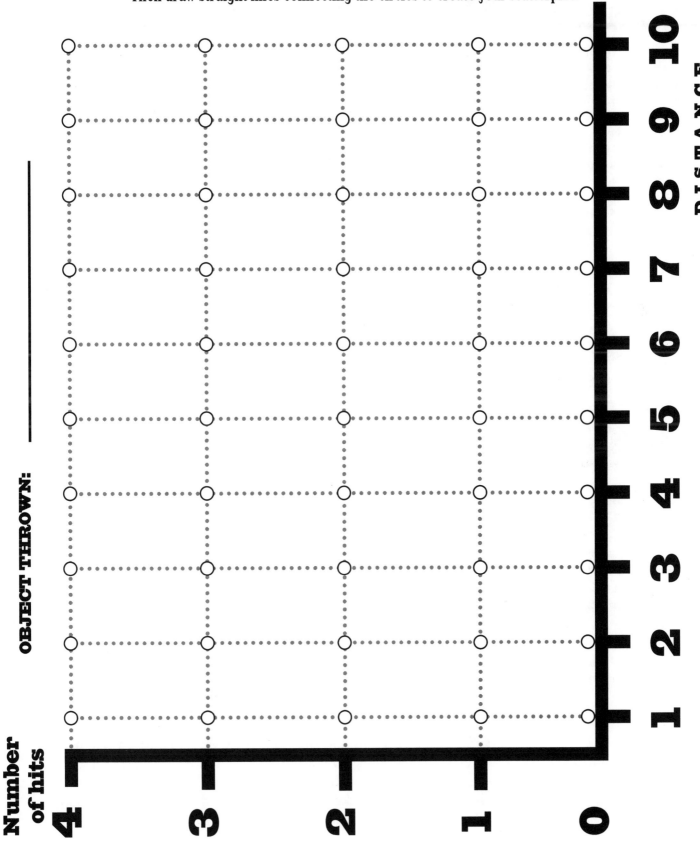

STORYLINE

Before the campfire is lit, young cowpokes go hunting for numbers that combine to make other numbers. Whoever captures the most cards gets the best grub. Yummy! Beans, ribs, and all the fixins!

CONCEPT CORRAL

NUMBER & OPERATION

➼ Find three or more numbers that add up to a third number.

➼ Create number sentences involving both addition and subtraction.

➼ Develop fluidity in addition and subtraction.

ALGEBRA

➼ Discover patterns in equivalent addition and subtraction sentences.

Hunting for Grub

GAME A
Cooperative/Competitive

GOAL: To find three or more numbers that add up to another number.

 # Players: 1, 2, 3, or 4 (can be played in a solitary fashion — a fun activity for children who finish assignments early).

1 Children are trying to collect as many cards as possible. At outset, educator sets goals linking number of cards collected to the four meal tickets, copied off master on p.21. Example: Educator might say that collecting 1 to 28 cards wins children a Barrel-Bottom Stew ticket; collecting 29 to 32 cards wins them a Young Rustler Leftover ticket; collecting 33 to 37 cards wins them a Scout Meal ticket; and collecting 38 or more wins them a Campfire Feast ticket.

2 Children shuffle cards and place deck face down. They take six cards off top of deck and place them face up in middle of table.

3a Children look at upturned cards, searching for three or more that add to any other. Example: If cards showing are: 1 2 3 4 6 & 10, children could add the 1, 2, and 3 to make 6, creating the number sentence: 1 + 2 + 3 = 6. Even better, they could make the number sentence: 1 + 2 + 3 + 4 = 10. Children take all cards in their number sentence and lay them to the side. Tell children that they want to use as many cards as possible in their number sentences. Educator may want children to write their number sentence on a sheet of paper. (See Tips & Pointers #2)

3b If children cannot make a number sentence with cards showing, each child takes a turn turning over one card at a time until children do find and make a number sentence.

4 As soon as children make a number sentence and take those cards, they take as many cards off top of deck as they used in their number sentence, and turn them face up. Then they try to make another number sentence with the new set of face-up cards.

5 Once children use all cards in deck, they count cards to see how many they collected. Based on how many they collected, they take the appropriate meal ticket, as described in Rule #1 above.

NOTE: To play this and the other two games competitively, each child takes a turn trying to make a number sentence. Whichever child collects most cards gets Campfire Feast ticket, whoever collects next most gets Scout Meal ticket, whoever gets third most cards gets Young Rustler Leftovers ticket; whoever collects least gets Barrel-Bottom Stew ticket.

GAME B
Cooperative/Competitive

GOAL: To make number sentences involving both addition and subtraction.

 # Players: 1, 2, 3, or 4.

Same rules as Game A with one challenging restriction. Now children must use **both** addition and subtraction in their number sentences. Example: If face-up cards are: **1   3   4   6   9   & 10**, children could make sentences like: $4 + 6 - 1 = 9$ or $10 + 3 - 4 = 9$. Note that children may work with sums higher than 10 (such as $10 + 3 = 13$ in the previous example) as long as their final answer is 10 or less. Also, players are free to use subtraction before addition, as in the sentence: $4 - 1 + 6 = 9$. And players may make sentences using more than four cards. In fact, they are encouraged to do so. Example: Players could make a sentence like: $3 + 4 + 9 - 6 = 10$

Again, children play for meal tickets.

GAME C
Cooperative/Competitive

GOAL: To make two number sentences that involve either addition or subtraction, or both addition and subtraction.

 # Players: 1, 2, 3, or 4.

Same basic play as in Games A and B, only now children have even more options. The guidelines for this game are that students must simply find two addition / subtraction expressions that equal each other. Here are some examples of the variety of number sentences possible:

➼ addition of two numbers on both sides: $2 + 5 = 3 + 4$

➼ addition of three numbers on both sides: $1 + 1 + 6 = 2 + 2 + 4$

➼ simple subtraction on both sides: $10 - 4 = 8 - 2$

➼ double subtraction on both sides: $10 - 2 - 3 = 8 - 1 - 2$

➼ addition on one side; subtraction on the other: $5 + 2 = 9 - 2$

➼ addition and subtraction on both sides: $8 - 3 + 1 = 10 - 8 + 4$

ROUNDUP

FOR EACH GROUP OF CHILDREN:

➼ **One deck with all picture cards removed. Ace stands for the number 1. If you wish, use Joker and let it stand for the number 0. Using the Joker here allows children to use facts like $7 + 2 + 0 = 9$ or $9 - 7 + 0 = 2$.**

➼ **Sample Games Layout sheet, copied off master on p.20. This sheet gives children a quick view of what kinds of number sentences they can form in each of the three games.**

➼ **Meal Tickets, copied off master on p.21. Photocopy enough meal tickets so that each group has several of each kind. Children can use these meal tickets to track their success.**

CAMPFIRE CHAT

1 Using cards from one deck, what is the greatest number of cards you can possibly take with one number sentence in Game A? **A: 8, for you could theoretically make this number sentence:**
1 + 1 + 1 + 1 + 2 + 2 + 2 = 10.

2 What is the lowest sum you can make in Game A? **A: Since you must use three addends, the lowest sum you can make is 3, by creating the number sentence: 1 + 1 + 1 = 3.**

* 3 What kinds of upturned cards make it easier to make a number sentence in Game A. Why? **A: A mixture of higher and lower cards, with more lower than higher. Lower cards serve as addends; higher cards serve as the sum.**

* 4 What kinds of upturned cards make it harder to make a number sentence in Game A? Why? **A: In general, high cards make it harder to make a sentence. In fact, you can never make a sentence if upturned cards are all 4 or higher, since 4 + 4 + 4 = 12, and you can't make a sum of 12 since the highest card you can use for the sum is 10.**

* 5 In Game B, does the order of numbers being added or subtracted ever matter? That is, do you get the same result if your number sentence says either: **4 + 2 − 3** or **2 + 4 − 3**? How about if you say: **4 − 2 + 3**? Why does the order matter sometimes but not other times? **A: The order doesn't matter as long as the same numbers are being added and subtracted. That is, 4 + 2 − 3 gives the same answer as 2 + 4 − 3 because in both sentences the 2 and 4 are being added, and the 3 is being subtracted. But in 4 − 2 + 3, the 4 and 3 are being added, and the 2 is being subtracted. Adding different numbers and subtracting different numbers can lead to different answers.**

6 In Game B, is there any limit to the number of cards you can use to make a number sentence? **A: The only limit is the number of cards you're playing with. For example, children could make a sentence like this: 1 − 1 + 2 − 2 + 3 − 3 + 4 − 4 + 5 − 5 + 6 − 6 + 7 − 7 + 8 − 8 + 9 − 9 + 10 − 10 + 1 = 1 (or even longer!)**

* 7 Did you notice any patterns when forming addition number sentences using two addends on each side in Game C? **A: Answers will vary, but here's one pattern some will notice. In sentences like: 1 + 7 = 2 + 6, the first addend goes up by one (from 1 to 2) while the second addend goes down by one (from 7 to 6), so there is a certain balance. This can be expressed algebraically as:**
$$a + b = (a + 1) + (b − 1).$$

Children can often grasp this if you substitute geometric symbols — like squares and circles — for "a" and "b."

*8 Did you notice any patterns when making subtraction number sentences using two numbers on each side in Game C? **A: Answers will vary, but here's one pattern some will notice. In sentences like: 10 – 4 = 8 – 2, both the first and second numbers go down by 2 (from 10 to 8, and from 4 to 2). So again, there is a certain balance. This can be expressed algebraically as:**

$$a - b = (a - 2) - (b - 2).$$

Children can often grasp this if you substitute geometric symbols — like squares and circles — for "a" and "b."

*9 Did you eventually find any ways to work with numbers more quickly in Game C? If so, can you describe the strategies you discovered? **A: Answers will vary.**

TIPS AND POINTERS

1 Model how to make number sentences before letting children play. Stress that in Games A and B, both the addends and the answer are to be found among the face-up cards. Stress that in Game C, all the numbers they need are found among the face-up cards.

2 Educator may want children to record their number sentences on a sheet of paper to keep track of the kinds of sentences they are making, and to monitor for computational accuracy.

3 In Game C, educator may wish to restrict the game to certain kinds of number sentences before allowing children to use all kinds permitted. For example, when starting out, educator might restrict children to number sentences with two numbers on each side, or to numbers sentences just involving addition, or to number sentences just involving subtraction. As children become more familiar with all the ways to make number sentences, educator can gradually remove restrictions.

4 Challenge Level: Once children become comfortable with Games A and B, add a fun twist by allowing them to make two or more different number sentences in one turn. Example: If upturned cards are: 2   3   4   6   7   &   10, children could make two number sentences on one turn: **2 + 4 = 6** and **3 + 7 = 10**, and thereby take all six cards on one turn!

Hunting for Grub
Sample Games Layout Master

Game A

Cards showing: 5♠ A♥ 7♦ 8♣ 2♥ 6♠

You can take: 5♠ A♥ 2♥ 8♣

Because ... 5♠ + 2♥ + A♥ = 8♣

Game B

Cards showing: 5♠ A♥ 7♦ 8♣ 2♥ 6♠

You can take: 5♠ 8♣ 6♠ 7♦

Because ... 5♠ + 8♣ − 7♦ = 6♠

Game C

Cards showing: 5♠ A♥ 7♦ 8♣ 2♥ 6♠

You can take: 5♠ A♥ 8♣ 2♥

Because ...   +   = −

Hunting for Grub
Meal Ticket Master

Campfire Feast

All you can eat of beans, bar-b-que ribs, honey-glazed prairie chicken, cornbread with orange marmalade, apple pie with ice cream, and hot chocolate too.

Scout Meal

A hefty plate of beans, a side of ribs, cornbread, and cowboy coffee (ground coffee beans in hot water).

Young Rustler Leftovers

Boiled pig's feet, a hunk of cornbread, a cold baked potato, and a tin cup full of hot water.

Barrel-Bottom Stew

A "tasty" mixture of hot water with rib and pig drippings.

STORYLINE

It's spring! Time for the yearly roundup contest. Cowpokes at rival ranches see who can round up the most cattle. In the first version of the contest, cowpokes try to round up 99 cattle as quickly as possible; in the other version, they try to round up 999 cattle!

CONCEPT CORRAL

NUMBER & OPERATION
➤ Use place value concepts to compare sizes of various numbers.

➤ Add numbers to increase sizes of numbers.

DATA ANALYSIS & PROBABILITY
➤ Think through answers to Campfire Chat questions.

REASONING
➤ Lay down cards in such a way as to create the largest number possible.

➤ Rearrange cards to create the largest number possible.

➤ Analyze which of two strategies is best to use in these games.

GAME A
Cooperative

GOAL: To round up as many as 99 cattle. Or as many as 999, in the variation.

 # Players: 1, 2, 3, or 4.

1 Children lay down the "99 Gameboard," copied off master on p.25. Children shuffle deck, place it face down, and turn over top card.

2 Children put the turned-over card in either the ones place or tens place of Gameboard. Example: If card is a 3, children may place it in the ones place, giving them a running total of 3; or they can put it in the tens place, giving them a running total of 30. Note that if no card is in the ones place, it's as if there's a zero there.

3 Children turn over next card and decide where to put it. Their choices: **a)** they can add second card to first card by placing it on top. e.g. Suppose first card is a 3, and children put it in the tens place. If second card is a 5, children may put this 5 on top of the 3, giving them a running total of 80, since the 3 + 5 equals 8 in tens place. **b)** Or, children can put the 5 in ones place, giving them a running total of 35 (3 in tens place, and 5 in ones place).

4 If a card cannot be used, it gets placed to the side. Example: Suppose children have 35 showing on Gameboard, and next card is a 7. They cannot add 7 to either the 3 or the 5, for it would make either pile's total exceed 9. Therefore this 7 gets placed to the side. Note: Children should not bury this card in the deck, for it will be used in the second part of the round, the "Rearranging" phase, described in Rule #6 below.

5 Children continue playing in this way until they have taken five cards. They record their total in the "Initial Number of Cows" column on Roundup Rivals Recording Sheet, copied off master on p.27.

6 After recording their initial score, children pick up their five cards and see if they can come up with a higher total by rearranging them however they wish. e.g. Suppose the 5 cards were turned over in this order: 7 - 2 - 4 - Ace - 5. Suppose children put them down so that their initial total was 95 (7 and 2 in the tens place; 4 and Ace in ones place; the 5 discarded). But when they take the cards off Gameboard and rearrange them, they keep the 7 and 2 in the tens place, but put the 4 and 5 in the ones place (now putting the Ace to the side), thereby getting the maximum possible total of 99!

7 After rearranging cards, children write down their rearranged score in the "Number of Cows After Rearranging" column on Roundup Rivals Recording Sheet.

Variation: Play this same game with the "999" Gameboard, copied off master on p.26. In this case, children take six cards per round.

GOAL: To beat rival ranchers by rounding up more cattle than they do — up to 99 in the first game, and up to 999 in the variation game.

 # Players: 2, or 4. With 2, play one against the other; with 4, play pair vs. pair.

Same basic play as in Game A, only now each child (or team of two children) plays against another child (or team of two), and each team gets its own Gameboard. Each team now tries to round up a greater number of cows than opposing team. As in Game A, there are two phases to each round. In Phase 1, children compete in rounding up the greater "Initial" number of cows. In Phase 2, they compete to round up the greater number of cows after "Rearranging." Scoring: to keep track of score, children take tokens from a bowl. A team takes one token for getting either the greater "Initial" number, or the greater "Rearranged" number. Thus, if a team rounds up both the greater "Initial" number and the greater "Rearranged" number, it takes two tokens on that round. If there is a tie for either the "Initial" or "Rearranged" number, neither team earns a token for that phase of the round. Play until one team earns 10 tokens. That team wins the Roundup Rivalry.

Variation: Play this competitive version with the "999" Gameboard. Each team gets six cards per round.

CAMPFIRE CHAT

1 On the "99 Gameboard," is it more important to build a large number in the ones place or in the tens place? And why? **A:** It's more important to build a large number in the tens place, for a larger number in the tens place makes a number larger, even if its ones digit is less. Example: Compare 61 and 59. The ones digit of 59 is greater than the ones digit of 61 (9 vs. 1). But because the tens digit of 61 is greater than the tens digit of 59 (6 vs. 5), 61 is greater than 59. Moral of the story: A larger tens digit ALWAYS BEATS a smaller tens digit, no matter what the ones digits may be.

2 On the "999 Gameboard," which digit is most important in determining the value of a number? Which is next most important? Which is least important? **A:** Hundreds digit is most important; tens digit is next most important; ones digit is least important.

3 The location where you place your first card makes a big difference in this game. For example, if you draw a 5, putting it in the tens place gives you 50, while putting it in the ones place gives you just 5. And 50 is 45 more than 5. So the "difference" between the two possible

ROUNDUP

FOR EACH CHILD OR GROUP:

➤ Deck with all Aces through 9s.

➤ One Roundup Rivals Gameboard, either the "99 Gameboard," copied off master on p.25; or the "999 Gameboard," copied off master on p.26. Note: use one Gameboard per group in the cooperative Game A; use one Gameboard per team or child in the competitive Game B.

➤ Roundup Rivals Recording Sheet, copied off master on p.27. One per group in Game A; one per child or team in Game B.

➤ Game B: Approximately 20 tokens in a bowl, for keeping score.

choices is 45. Which card allows you the greatest difference on the first turn, and what is that difference? Which card allows you the least difference on the first turn, and what is that? **A: 9 allows the greatest difference. 90 – 9 = a difference of 81 cows. Ace (1) allows you the least difference. 10 – 1 = a difference of just 9 cows.**

4 Does it sometimes pay off to put your first card(s) in the tens place? **A: Yes, here's an example using the "99 Gameboard." Suppose the cards in the deck — unbeknownst to you — are in the following order: Ace - 2 - 4 - 3 - 2. If you place the first three cards in the ones place (holding out for a high card in the tens place), you end up with a paltry "Initial" roundup of just 57 cows (Ace + 2 + 4 = 7 in ones place; 3 + 2 = 5 in tens place). Had you instead placed the first three cards in the tens place, you would have had a heftier roundup of 75 cows (Ace + 2 + 4 = 7 in tens place, and 3 + 2 = 5 in ones place).**

5 Does it sometimes pay off to wait on putting a card in the tens place? **A: Yes, given a certain arrangement of cards, it can pay off to wait a bit before putting a card in the tens place. Suppose your cards are in this order: 2 - 4 - 9 - Ace - 5. If you first put cards in tens place , you get an "Initial" roundup of 79 cows (2 & 4, then Ace in tens place, 9 in ones place. But if you wait, you can get an "Initial" roundup of 97 cows (2, 4, and Ace in ones place, 9 in tens place). The problem is that you can't know the order of your cards in advance!**

* 6 Given the two possible strategies described in questions 4 and 5 above, which of the two strategies do you think is better overall? And why? **A: Answers will vary.**

* 7 Focus on one game you played. Explain how you placed your five or six cards, and tell why. Explain what changes you made — and why — when you rearranged your cards. **A: Answers will vary.**

TIPS AND POINTERS

1 It's a good idea to model this game on an overhead projector or table-top before children play. Help children understand that they add the cards in each pile together to get the single digit for that place value. e.g. If they put a 4 and a 2 in the tens place, that stands for 60, since 4 + 2 = 6. And if they put a 4 and a 2 in the hundreds place, that stands for 600.

2 Model situations in which a card must be placed to the side. It's important for children to realize that once they put a card on Gameboard, they cannot remove it until the time for rearranging arrives. (Some children are tempted to get rid of the cards they have laid down as soon as they get a 9.)

3 It also helps to model how to fill out the Roundup Rivals Recording Sheet.

Tens Place

Ones Place

Roundup Rivals
"999" Gameboard Master

Ones Place

Tens Place

Hundreds Place

Roundup Rivals
Recording Sheet Master

Game 1

Initial Number of Cows	Number of Cows After Rearranging

Game 2

Initial Number of Cows	Number of Cows After Rearranging

Just as a Rancher sits down to supper, a steer breaks out of its pen. The Rancher has to chase it up and down the ranchland, and the Steer tries to get away through a "Broken Fence." Will the Rancher capture the Steer, or will the Steer make it to freedom?

CONCEPT CORRAL

NUMBER & OPERATION
➤ Add integers using a number line.

ALGEBRA
➤ Develop foundation for concept of positive and negative numbers by moving tokens through northern spaces (positive numbers), across the zero space, and into southern spaces (negative spaces).
➤ Add positive and negative integers.

PROBLEM SOLVING
➤ Develop and test strategies for winning.

CONNECTIONS
➤ See ties between moving along a number line and adding positive and negative integers.

Steer on the Loose!

GAME A Competitive

GOAL: For the Rancher, to catch the Steer. For the Steer, to reach freedom through the "Broken Fence."

 # Players: 2, or 4. With 2, play one vs. one; with 4, play pair vs. pair.

1 Both decks are shuffled and placed face down on Steer on the Loose! Card Layout Sheet: black cards on the "Black Pile" space, red cards on the "Red Pile" space. One child chooses to be Steer, other child chooses to be Rancher. If four play, one pair can be the Steer and make decisions together, and in same way other pair can be Rancher.

2 Rancher and Steer both place one token on the **0** position in their respective lanes.

3 Whichever player is Steer chooses a card from either black or red pile. If player chooses a **black** card, she moves her token as many spaces **up** as indicated by number on card. e.g **Black 3** tells her to move token **3 spaces up** — to the **+3** space. If she chooses chooses a **red** card, she moves token as many spaces **down** as indicated by number on card. e.g. **Red 2** tells her to move token **2 spaces down** — to the **-2** space.

4 After Steer moves, Rancher picks one card from either pile with goal of landing on same position that Steer is now on.

5 Rancher and Steer alternate moves. Steer tries to reach either the **+10** or **-10** space, for if she arrives at either of those spaces, she gains freedom through the "Broken Fence." Rancher wins by landing on same space that Steer is on — or if Steer lands on same space that Rancher is on.

6 If either deck runs out of cards, children shuffle that deck and resume play. This way children can always choose a card from either deck.

1 Who won more at your game: the Steer, or the Rancher? **A: Answers will vary, but game is designed so that the chances of winning are about 50-50.**

2 If you want to move up, from what deck should you draw cards? **A: From the black deck.**

3 If you want to move down, from what deck should you draw cards? **A: From the red deck.**

*4 When you were the Steer, did you ever start out heading for one "Broken Fence," then turn around and head for the other "Broken Fence"? If so, why? **A: Steer should realize that if she is at first ahead of Rancher heading north or south, but then Rancher passes her in that direction, she is better off changing directions. That way she cannot accidentally run into Rancher on next turn. Example: On first move, Steer draws a black 2. Then Rancher draws a black 3. Playing smart, Steer should switch directions and draw a red card, for by so doing she can't accidentally run into Rancher.**

 TIPS AND POINTERS

1 To let children play more and shuffle less, use cards from three decks when creating the black and red piles. With this set-up, black pile contains six black Aces, six black 2s, six black 3s, and two black 4s. Red pile contains six red Aces, six red 2s, six red 3s, and two red 4s.

2 Model game on an overhead or at a desk before children play. It's important to show them how to move their pieces.

3 To highlight algebraic element of the game, have children record moves on Move-Recording worksheet, copied off master on p.32. To use worksheet, show children that they write number of space their token is on in first rectangle. Then they write number of card they draw in second rectangle (black cards being positive; red cards being negative). Finally they record number of space they land on in third rectangle. In this way, children can record number sentences like: $+2 + (-4) = -2$. Best of all, they can see what this means on the Gameboard!

4 If you use Move-Recording worksheet, it helps to copy it onto both sides of a sheet so children have ample space to record moves.

5 If you plan to ask Campfire Chat Question #1, have children keep track of how many times Rancher and Steer wins.

ROUNDUP

FOR EACH PAIR OR GROUP OF PLAYERS:

➤ One pile with three red Aces (i.e. any combination of hearts or diamonds), three red 2s, three red 3s, and one red 4. Similarly, one pile with three black Aces (i.e. any combination of spades or clubs), three black 2s, three black 3s, and one black 4.

➤ Note that you'll need cards from two decks to assemble these piles, but it's worth it!

➤ One Steer on the Loose! Card Layout Sheet from master on p.30 for every pair or group. Children may discard this sheet once they get a feel for the card layout.

➤ One Steer on the Loose! Gameboard, copied off master on p.31, for every pair or group.

➤ Two tokens to move on Gameboard.

➤ OPTIONAL: Move-Recording worksheet, copied off master on p.32.

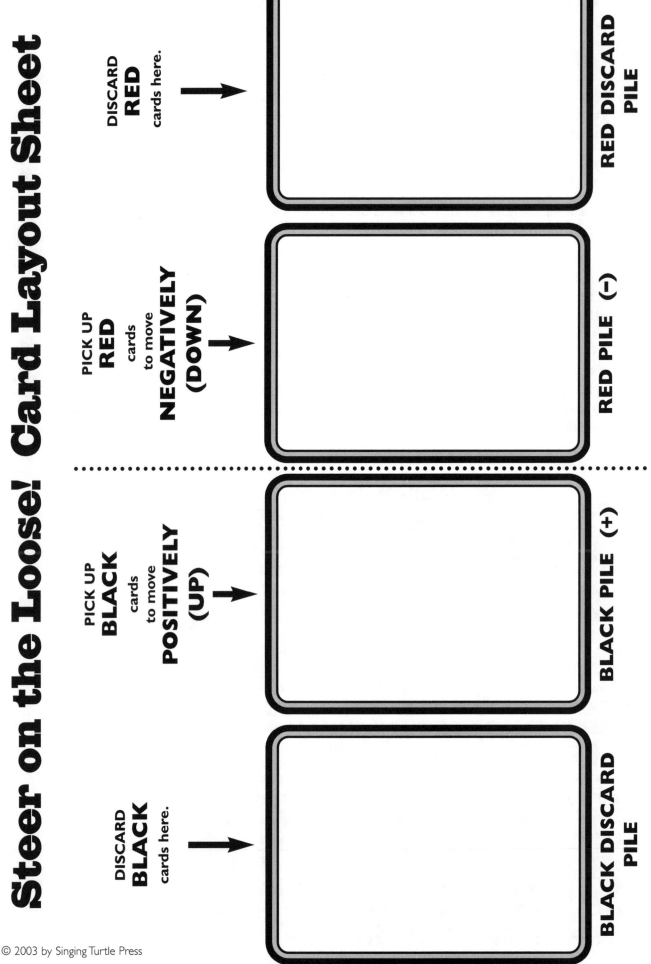

Steer on the Loose! Card Layout Sheet

DISCARD **RED** cards here. →

PICK UP **RED** cards to move **NEGATIVELY (DOWN)** →

PICK UP **BLACK** cards to move **POSITIVELY (UP)** →

DISCARD **BLACK** cards here. →

RED DISCARD PILE

RED PILE (−)

BLACK PILE (+)

BLACK DISCARD PILE

+ 10	+ 10
+ 9	+ 9
+ 8	+ 8
+ 7	+ 7
+ 6	+ 6
+ 5	+ 5
+ 4	+ 4
+ 3	+ 3
+ 2	+ 2
+ 1	+ 1
0	0
– 1	– 1
– 2	– 2
– 3	– 3
– 4	– 4
– 5	– 5
– 6	– 6
– 7	– 7
– 8	– 8
– 9	– 9
– 10	– 10

STEER

RANCHER

Steer on the Loose! Gameboard

Steer on the Loose!
Move-Recording Worksheet Master

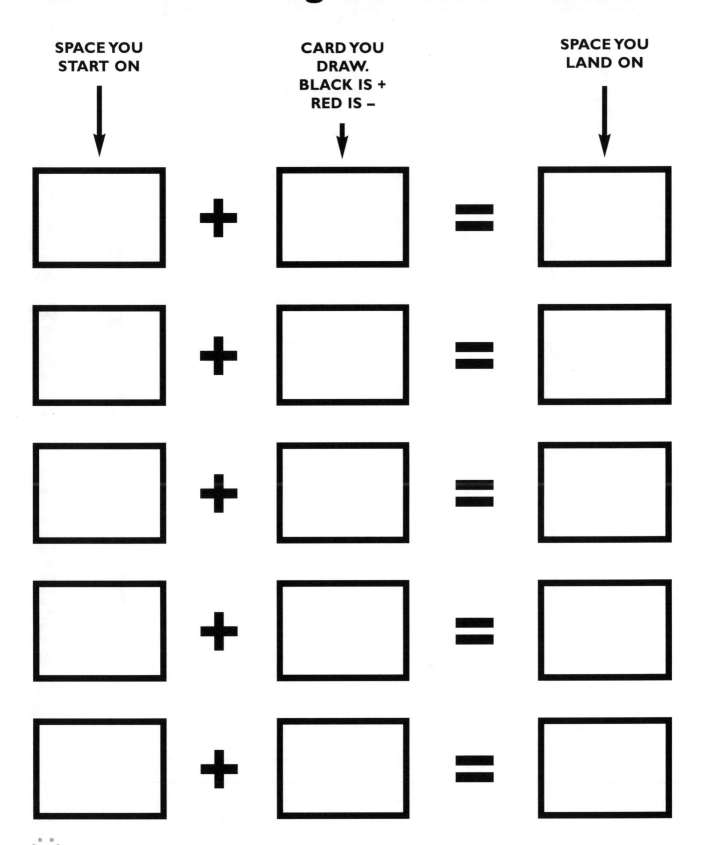

SPACE YOU
START ON

CARD YOU
DRAW.
BLACK IS +
RED IS –

SPACE YOU
LAND ON

A Traveling Circus moves through the West, entertaining cowpokes. One of the more popular circus performers is the Rattlesnake Reader, who can accurately guess the exact length of any rattlesnake. Buckaroos are invited to compete with the Rattlesnake Reader to see if they can read a snake's length as accurately as he can.

CONCEPT CORRAL

MEASUREMENT
➤ Compare lengths in inches, feet, yards, metric units. Estimate lengths.

REASONING
➤ Develop strategies for estimating lengths.

➤ Find everyday objects whose lengths are close to certain specified lengths.

REPRESENTATION
➤ Create "snakes" out of classroom materials (links, paper clips, linking cubes, etc.) that are a specified number of inches long.

Sizing up Snakes

GAME A
Cooperative

GOAL: Cowpokes measure lengths of string. Then they exchange pieces of string with one another and try to accurately guess their lengths. Finally, they find everyday objects with the same lengths as their pieces of string.

 # Players: 2, or 4. With 2, each child measures out a length of string, and the two of them exchange strings; with 4, pairs of children measure out lengths of string, and the two pairs exchange strings.

1 Each child (or pair of children) draws two cards from deck. Child adds cards to get a specific length for her "rattlesnake." e.g. If she draws a 5 and a 9, she adds these numbers to get 14". (See Tips & Pointers #3 for more advanced options.)

2 Child takes string and uses a ruler to measure out a snake (piece of string) the same length as the number found in Step 1.

3 Child cuts her string to correct length. e.g. She cuts a piece of string 14" long.

4 Then she and her partner exchange their pieces of string, not telling each other how long they are.

5 Each child now guesses the length of the piece of string she was given and writes her guess in "Guess" space on Sizing Up Snakes Game A Worksheet, copied off master on p.37. Encourage children to lay their pieces of string straight before making guesses.

6 Each child measures her piece of string and records both its actual length and the number of inches by which guess and actual length differ. e.g. If guess was 16" and actual length is 14", child writes 2" in "Difference" space on worksheet. Once children gain skill at estimating length, educator may want to award them points for guesses that are close to or equal to actual length.

7 OPTIONAL BUT FUN: Each partner/team searches for something in room that equals length of their string and records that in "Object" space on worksheet.

**GAME B**
Cooperative

GOAL: Each cowpoke creates a "rattlesnake" of links, trying to make its length as close as possible to a Goal Length. Each child then checks to see how close the length of her snake is to the Goal Length.

 # Players: 1, 2, 3, or 4. Children may work independently or together.

1 Children gather manipulatives that fit together (e.g. linking cubes, links, paper clips, paper links, etc.).

2 Children select two cards from deck and add their numbers together. The sum of those cards is the Goal Length for "rattlesnake" to be made. e.g. If two cards are a 10 and a 7, snake to be made is 17" long. Children write this number in "Goal Length" space on Sizing up Snakes Game B Worksheet, copied off master on p.37.

3 Without using a ruler or any measuring device, children create a rattlesnake of linking manipulatives whose length is as close as they can make it to Goal Length.

4 Children then measure their snake to see how close its length is to Goal Length. They write its measurement in "Actual Length" space on worksheet.

5 Children calculate difference between Goal Length and Actual Length, and write that number in "Difference" space on worksheet.

6 Once children gain skill at this exercise, educator may wish to award children points for creating snakes that are close to or equal to Goal Lengths.

ROUNDUP

FOR EACH PAIR OR GROUP:

➻ **Deck with all Aces through 10s.**

➻ **String and scissors. Note: In using string, avoid yarn, as it stretches and therefore cannot be measured precisely.**

➻ **Links, linking cubes, paper clips, or other manipulatives that can be linked together.**

➻ **One-foot rulers, yardsticks, or meter sticks.**

➻ **Sizing up Snakes Worksheet, copied off master on p.37.**

CAMPFIRE CHAT

1 Do you find it is easier to estimate shorter or longer lengths? And why? **A: Answers will vary, but most students find shorter lengths easier to estimate than longer lengths.**

2 Once you know the length of an object, might it help to look at that object when guessing the length of a different object? **A: Most students find that it does help to look at objects whose lengths they know when estimating lengths of other objects. They may even talk about how previously measured strings provide useful comparisons.**

3 Does playing this game help you guess how long something is without measuring it? **A: Most children say yes because their guesses**

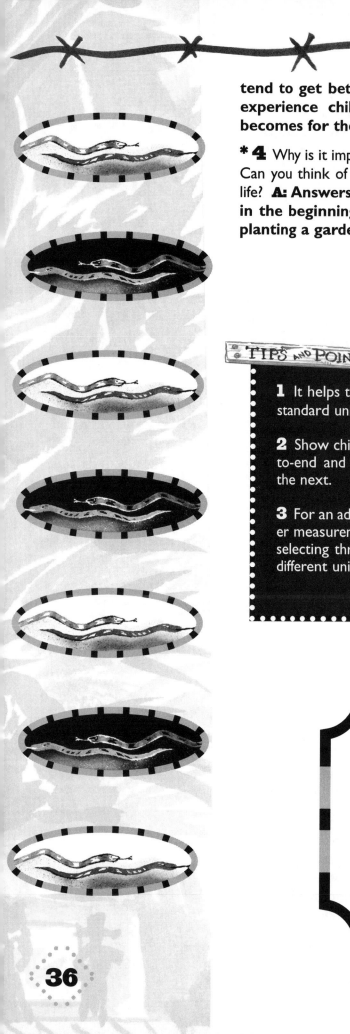

tend to get better the longer they play the game. The more experience children have with measurement, the easier it becomes for them to make reasonable guesses about length.

*4 Why is it important to be able to make good guesses about length? Can you think of some ways you might use this skill in your everyday life? **A: Answers will vary, but some possible answers might be: in the beginning stages of building projects, buying furniture, planting a garden, cutting brownies.**

TIPS AND POINTERS

1 It helps to have children explore measurement with non-standard units before moving into inches, feet, and yards.

2 Show children how they may place several 12" rulers end-to-end and thereby continue measuring from one ruler to the next.

3 For an additional challenge, children who master the smaller measurements allowed for by two cards may move up to selecting three or four cards each turn — or working with different units (e.g. half inches, centimeters, etc.).

Sizing up Snakes
Worksheet Master

Game A Worksheet

Guess	Actual Length	Difference	Object

●●●

Game B Worksheet

Goal Length	Actual Length	Difference

37

CONCEPT CORRAL

NUMBER & OPERATION
➤ Add and subtract numbers.

ALGEBRA
➤ Learn patterns for adding and subtracting two numbers, based on whether they are odd or even.

➤ Learn patterns for adding three numbers, based on whether they are odd or even.

Battle for Cattle

GAME A
Competitive

GOAL: To win more cows than the other Rancher by finding pairs that add up to an even or to an odd number.

 # Players: 2, or 4. (With 2, play one vs. one; with 4, play pair vs. pair.)

1 Children shuffle and place deck face down. One player picks a card from deck without looking at it. If card's number is even, that player becomes the Even Rancher, and other player becomes the Odd Rancher; and vice-versa. Card is returned to deck. Whichever player didn't pick the card gets to be dealer.

2 Dealer places the four cards on top of deck face up between the two Ranchers (players or teams). These cards represent the cows with odd and even brands.

3 Non-dealer studies the four cards, trying to find one or two pairs whose brands add up to **a)** an even number, if he is the Even Rancher, or **b)** an odd number, if he is the Odd Rancher.

4a If first player does find one or two pairs, he puts those cards by his side, for these are the "cows" he has won on that round. Dealer then puts out as many cards as first player took, and dealer gets to take a similar turn. Since dealer always puts back as many cards as were taken, there are always four cards available for use on each player's turn.

4b If either player cannot make a pair on his turn, it becomes the other player's turn to try to make a pair with those same four cards.

5 Play continues in this way until all cards in deck are used.

6 At the end, each player counts his cards. Whoever has more cards has taken more cows, and this player is the winner of that round.

Variation: Instead of having children add their cards to get sums, have them subtract cards to get differences that are either odd or even.

 **GAME B** **Competitive**

GOAL: To win more cows than the other Rancher by finding sets of three cards that add up to an even or odd number.

 # Players: 2, or 4. (With 2, play one vs. one; with 4, play pair vs. pair.)

Same basic game as Game A, with these two differences:

a) Dealer now lays out six cards before each turn.

b) Players MUST take THREE cards to win cows. e.g. Suppose cards laid out are: Ace, 2, 4, 7, 9, and 10, and it is Even Rancher's turn. Even Rancher could take the Ace, 2, and 7, for **1 + 2 + 7 = 10**, an even number. Similarly, Even Rancher could take any of these other sets of three cards that add up to even numbers: Ace, 2, 9 / Ace, 4, 7 / Ace, 4, 9 / Ace, 7, 10 / or Ace, 9, 10.

 CAMPFIRE CHAT

1 If one player cannot take any cards on his turn, does that mean that the other player definitely can take cards on his turn? **A: Yes, if the Odd Rancher cannot make a set on his turn, it means that the sums of the cards must all be even. So the Even Rancher must be able to make two sums on his turn.**

*2 Did you see any patterns in Game A for adding and subtracting odd and even numbers? If so, what patterns did you see? **A: Children should see the following patterns:**

even + even = even
odd + odd = even
even + odd = odd
odd + even = odd

even − even = even
odd − odd = even
even − odd = odd
odd − even = odd

Generalization: When the two cards that you are adding or subtracting are both even or both odd, the answer is even. When the two cards you are adding or subtracting are mixed — one even, one odd — the answer is odd.

*3 Did you see any patterns in Game B for adding and subtracting odd and even numbers? If so, what patterns did you see? **A: Children should see the following patterns:**

3 evens = even
2 evens & 1 odd = odd
2 odds & 1 even = even
3 odds = odd

*4 In Game A, does either the Even Rancher or the Odd Rancher have an advantage? If so, how do you know? Hint: Think of the various ways you can make an even or an odd number. **A: This is a tough question, but some children can see that the Even Rancher has a slight advantage. There are five basic ways that the four cards will show up: a) all even, b) three even, one odd, c) two even, two odd, d) one even, three odd, e) all odd. It turns out that two of those five ways favor the Even Rancher: (a) all even, and (e) all odd. These layouts favor the Even Rancher because he can make two pair of even sums, while the Odd Rancher can make no pair of odd sums.**

40

Battle for Cattle
Sample Games Layout Master

Game A

It's Even Rancher's turn, and the cards showing are ...

Even Rancher takes ...

because 4 + 6 = 10, an even number.

It's Odd Rancher's turn, and the cards showing are ...

Odd Rancher takes ...

because 8 + 1 = 9, an odd number.

Game B

It's Even Rancher's turn, and the cards showing are ...

Even Rancher takes ...

because 5 + 7 + 10 = 22, an even number.

It's Odd Rancher's turn, and the cards showing are ...

Odd Rancher takes ...

because 6 + 2 + 9 = 17, an odd number.

Quicksand

GAME A — Competitive

GOAL: To find safety by reaching the Tree Branch, or to be the one player who has not fallen into the Quicksand Pit after all others have fallen in.

> **# Players:** 2, 3, or 4. With 4, play pair vs. pair.

1 Shuffle deck, place it face down, and lay it where everyone may take cards off the top. Each player puts a token on space 7 on any of the four pathways of Gameboard, copied off master on p.45.

2 First player takes top card and turns it over. Card's number tells how many spaces to move; card's suit color tells which direction to move in. Move DOWN — toward Quicksand Pit — if suit is RED. Move UP — toward Tree Branch — if suit is BLACK.

3 If player reaches the 14 space, she is rescued by grabbing onto the Tree Branch and stops playing. Play continues for other players.

4 Two ways to win, and more than one player may win: **a)** if a child gets to safety by reaching the Tree Branch, or **b)** if all the other players have fallen into the Quicksand Pit and a child is last player left.

5 When children run out of cards, they shuffle deck to ensure they don't repeat the last run of cards, then continue playing.

GAME B — Cooperative

GOAL: Children work as a team, trying to get all four cowhands to safety by forming a human chain with tokens on spaces 14, 13, 12, and 11. Idea is that cowhand on 14 grabs onto the Tree Branch, and each cowhand below hangs onto legs of cowhand above. Hang on tight!

> **# Players:** 1, 2, 3, or 4 (this is a fun solitaire game, too).

DECK DIFFERENCE: See Roundup.
CONCEPTUAL DIFFERENCE: In Game A children identify with a particular token, but in Game B children do not identify with any token. Rather, their goal is to cooperate in managing tokens so all four cowhands (tokens) reach safety at the Tree Branch.

1 Children place one token on space **7** on each of the four pathways.

There must be four tokens on the board.

2 For the team to win, the four tokens must end up on spaces 14, 13, 12, and 11, and they may arrive at those spaces in any order.

3 Players turn over cards one at a time. As each card is turned over, children confer to decide which of the four tokens would be best to move by number and direction indicated on card (same rule as in Game A: BLACK suits move tokens UP, RED suits move tokens DOWN).

4 Children may move any of the tokens on any turn. Children do not need to move tokens in any particular order. Strategy lies in deciding which token to move on any turn.

5 Even after a token has reached one of the spaces from 11 through 14, children may move it if they so wish. This makes it easier for them to avoid having a token fall into Quicksand Pit.

6 If card drawn would seemingly make a token overshoot space 14, token goes to space 14. Example: Token is on 12, and children draw a black 3 — technically, token should go on 15, but as there is no 15, it goes on 14.

7 Team wins only if every token gets to safety by being in a chain from 11 through 14. If three tokens reach safety but the fourth falls into Quicksand Pit, everyone loses.

Challenge Level for Game B: (two restrictions)

a) Tokens must arrive in order from Tree Branch on down. That is, first one token must arrive on space 14, then one on space 13, then one on on space 12, finally one on space 11.

b) Once children put token on space 14, it is "locked" and can no longer move in any direction. Similarly, once a token is on space 14 and a second token lands on space 13, token on 13 gets locked. Same for a token moving to space 12 after tokens are locked on 13 and 14. Children may want to turn tokens over to show that they are locked. Note: It's o.k. for a token to land on a space where another token is locked. That is, if tokens are locked on 14 and 13, another token may land on 14 or 13; it just won't get locked there. There's a much greater chance of losing in this game until children learn some smart strategies!

ROUNDUP

FOR EACH GROUP OF CHILDREN:

➤ One Quicksand Gameboard, copied off master on p.45.

➤ In Game A, one token per player for the Gameboard (small buttons work well). In Game B, you'll need four tokens, no matter how many children are playing.

➤ Game A: One deck with all Aces, 2s, 3s, and 4s.

➤ Game B: Same as Game A deck, but remove 4 of hearts and 4 of diamonds. OPTIONAL: Add one black 5 to the deck (5 of clubs or 5 of spades, but not both) if you want play to proceed faster.

1 In Game A, how can you tell if you might win or lose on the next card? In other words, how can you tell if you're in the "Danger Zone"? **A: You're in the "Danger Zone" if you are on space 1, 2, 3, or 4. That's because any red card could plunge you into the Quicksand Pit.**

2 In Game A, how can you tell if you might win on the next card? In other words, how can you tell if you're in the "Safety Zone"? **A: You're in the "Safety Zone" if you are on space 10, 11, 12, or 13. That's because any black card could allow you to reach the Tree Branch.**

3 The cooperative game's deck has more black cards than red cards. What effect does this have on the game? **A: The design of the deck makes it slightly more likely that you'll pick a card that moves you up than a card that moves you down.**

* 4 In the cooperative game, did you try any strategies that backfired? Why do you think they didn't work? **A: Children eventually realize that getting just one cowhand to safety while ignoring the others can be risky. In this situation, one of the cowhands may fall into the Quicksand Pit.**

* 5 In the cooperative game, did you eventually discover any good strategies? What made those work? **A: Children eventually realize that it's best to gradually move all of the cowhands toward the Tree Branch. That way, no cowhand will accidentally fall into the Pit.**

* 6 Did playing the Challenge Level of the cooperative game make play even harder? If so, how? **A: Children should realize that when tokens get locked, the remaining tokens face more danger of falling into the Pit.**

* 7 Did you eventually develop any winning strategies for the Challenge Level? If so, describe them. **A: Children usually realize that they should gradually move all tokens up toward the Tree Branch and lock tokens only when other tokens are out of the "Danger Zone."**

TIPS AND POINTERS

1 Demonstrate how to move tokens before letting children play. Stress that children count the number of moves they make, but NOT the space they start on (a common mistake for young counters). So if they are on **7** and draw a black 2, they count one for moving from **7** to **8**, and they count one for moving from **8** to **9**. The fact is: **7 + 2 = 9**.

2 Since this game lays a foundation for the number line concept, you may want to follow up with a number line lesson. If you've already introduced the number line, this game provides a fun, follow-up / reinforcement activity.

3 You may want children to state math facts either before or after they move tokens. This keeps emphasis of game on math facts, not just on moving tokens. Example: If a player is at **10** and draws a black 3, she says: **10 + 3 = 13**. If the player is at **10** and draws a red 4, he says: **10 – 4 = 6**. Players may either move, then say the fact; or say the fact, then move. You may also want children to write facts on a sheet of paper as they play.

4 Write this somewhere everyone can see it: **BLACK means + / RED means –** . Or for those who think more visually: **BLACK means UP / RED means DOWN.**

5 If you have enough cards, double deck size by using same cards from two decks. This allows play to continue longer between shufflings.

6 Game A is a fun warm-up. Game B raises the thinking to a more challenging level.

7 If children have trouble winning in Game B, you might suggest that they gradually move all their tokens up toward Tree Branch, rather than quickly moving one toward Branch. That way they have less risk of leaving behind one token that could fall into Quicksand Pit.

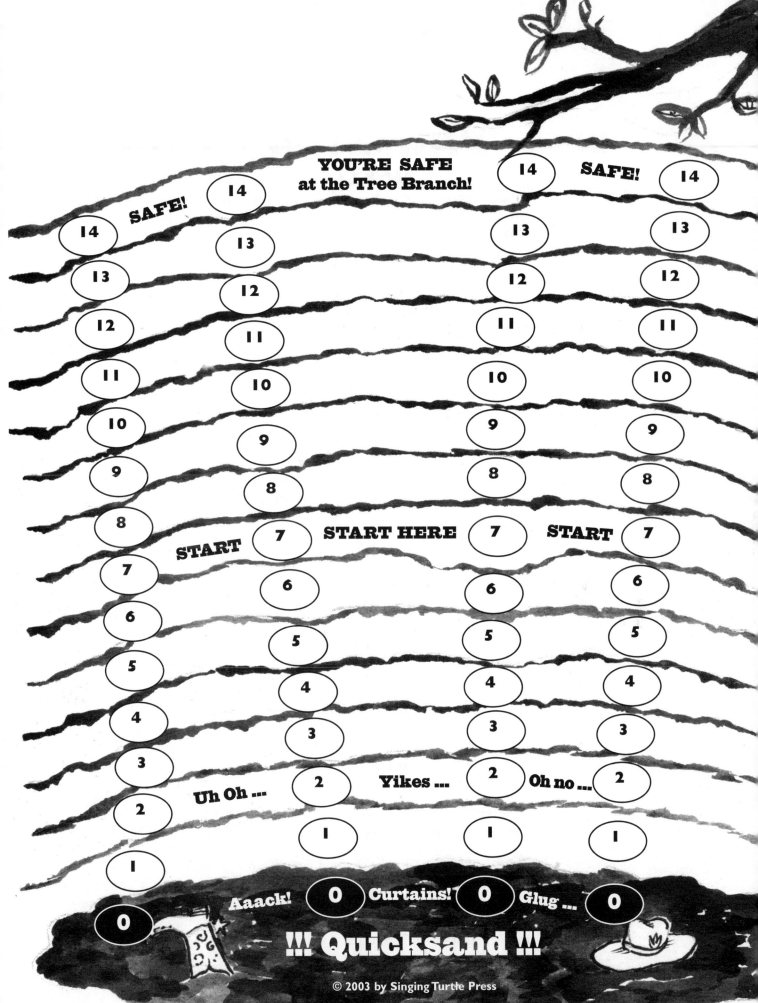

While training his new partner, Cowboy Casey, Buckaroo Bob teaches Casey Rule #1 — when placing steer in a corral, those steer must have something in common. After Casey learns this rule, Buckaroo Bob's mischievous streak leads him to play tricks on Casey. Will Buckaroo Bob out-wit Casey? Or can Casey figure out Bob's tricks? You'll have to play to find out.

CONCEPT CORRAL

ALGEBRA

➤ Assemble cards with a common attribute.

➤ Identify the common attribute of a group of cards.

➤ Determine which objects belong to a set and which objects do not belong.

PROBLEM SOLVING

➤ Figure out what attribute(s) defines a set.

REASONING

➤ Figure out why some cards belong to a set, while others do not belong.

The Bum Steer

GAME A
Cooperative/Competitive

GOAL: For Buckaroo Bob, to teach Cowboy Casey how to put the same kind of steer in a corral. For Cowboy Casey, to add one steer that belongs to the corral.

 # Players: 2, or 4.

1 Children split into "Buckaroo Bob" Team and "Cowboy Casey" Team (with 4 children, split 2 vs. 2; with 2 children, split 1 vs. 1). Children spread out all cards from a deck, laying them all face up. Buckaroo Bob Team makes circle with piece of yarn or toothpicks. This is the corral.

2 Buckaroo Bob Team confers and secretly chooses an attribute to unify its steer (see Tips & Pointers #2 for examples). Looking through deck, team finds three steer (cards) with this attribute and lays them face up inside corral.

3 Cowboy Casey Team studies the three steer and tries to determine the unifying attribute. Once it has an idea, it searches deck for another steer (card) that belongs and present it to Buckaroo Bob Team.

4 Buckaroo Bob Team tells whether or not steer presented belongs. If so, it gets placed face up inside corral along with other cards in the set. If not, it is placed face up, but outside corral.

5 As soon as Casey Team thinks it is certain of unifying attribute, it makes a guess, saying what attribute is. e.g. "All steer in the corral are clubs."

6a If guess is correct, teams switch roles and game continues.

6b If guess is incorrect, Bob Team says so, and to offer hint, finds and puts out one card that either belongs to set or does not belong — inside or outside corral — as appropriate. Then Casey Team confers and presents another card, and play continues until Casey Team states the unifying attribute.

7 After children play several times, they may want to document in their math journal their favorite set of steer — or present it to the class.

Variation: Same play as in Game A, only now Buckaroo Bob Team puts three PAIR of steer in the corral, each PAIR having a common attribute. Cowboy Casey tries to add a PAIR of steer with this same attribute to the corral. See Tips & Pointers #3 for examples of attributes that can unite a PAIR of cards.

GOAL: For Buckaroo Bob, to trick Cowboy Casey by placing four steer in the corral, one of which does not belong. For Casey, to figure out which steer does not belong. This is the "bum steer."

 # Players: 1, 2, 3, or 4.

1 Buckaroo Bob Team selects three cards with a common attribute and one card that does not have this attribute. This one card that does not belong is the "bum steer." Bob Team places all four cards face up in the corral. Example: 4 of diamonds, 2 of clubs, 7 of diamonds, 10 of diamonds (the 2 of clubs is the "bum steer," for it is the one card that is not a diamond).

2 Once the cards are laid out, Cowboy Casey Team tries to figure out which card is the "bum steer."

3 As soon as Casey Team thinks it knows which card is the "bum steer," it identifies the common attribute and tells which card it thinks does not belong. Children might say, for example: "All of the cards are diamonds, except for the 2 of clubs, so it is the 'bum steer.'"

4 If Casey Team is right, it gets one point and takes a token to keep track of its score.

5 If Casey Team is wrong, Bob Team must give a hint in either of two ways. It can either put another card that does belong into the corral, or it can select a card that does not belong and place it outside the corral.

6 Casey Team gets to have three hints. If it can't identify the "bum steer" after the third hint, Bob Team tells which is the "bum steer" and why. If Bob Team stumps Casey Team, Bob Team gets one point and takes a token to keep track of its score.

7 Whether Casey Team does or does not correctly identify the "bum steer," teams switch roles and play continues. Play 6 rounds. Whichever team gains more points wins.

Variation: Same play as in Game B, only now Bob Team puts three PAIR of steer in the corral, each PAIR having a common attribute, and one PAIR that does not share this attribute. Casey Team tries to figure out which PAIR of steer does NOT belong. See Tips & Pointers #3 for examples of attributes that can unite a PAIR of cards.

CAMPFIRE CHAT

1 What strategies did the Cowboy Casey Team use to figure out the attribute that unites the set of steer? **A: Answers will vary, but children's answers will reveal how well they understand the idea of attributes.**

ROUNDUP

FOR EACH GROUP OF CHILDREN:

➤ Deck with all Aces through 10s, plus the Jokers, which stand for the number zero.

➤ Piece of yarn or string that serves as the corral. You can also use a bunch of toothpicks, formed into a corral shape.

➤ Tokens for keeping score.

➤ The Bum Steer Sample Games Layout sheet, copied off master on p.49. Letting children see this sheet gives them an overview of how the games work.

2 As the Buckaroo Bob Team, did you ever have any trouble finding a card that did not belong? If so, describe what happened. **A: Answers will vary.**

* 3 When you were the Cowboy Casey Team, did you ever pick a card that you were sure was a "bum steer," yet it was not the one that the other team had in mind? How did you work out this situation? **A: Answers will vary, but children's responses will indicate whether or not they had trouble defining a set or grasping the concept of a set.**

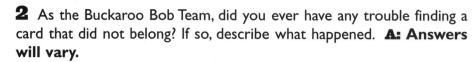

1 Children often like to make a gate in the corral, by which they can lead out "the bum steer." They can make the gate by arranging the yarn — or a toothpick — to swing open like a gate.

2 Examples of attributes Buckaroo Bob can use to form his SET of steer in Game A or Game B:

➼ same suit (e.g. spades); same number (e.g. the 4s); even numbered cards; odd numbered cards; cards with red suits; cards with black suits; cards less than a certain number (e.g. cards less than 4) cards greater than a certain number (e.g. cards greater than 7); cards within a certain range (e.g. cards between 4 and 7); even clubs; odd hearts; spades between 3 and 8; diamonds 5 and less; etc.

3 Examples of attributes Bob can use to form his PAIRS of steer for the variations to Game A and Game B:

➼ cards one apart (a 3 and a 4; a 6 and a 7; a 9 and a 10 — "bum steer" might be a 5 and a 7)

➼ cards two apart (a 5 and a 7; a 7 and a 9; an Ace and a 3 — "bum steer" might be a 6 and a 10)

➼ cards of the same suit (two clubs; two diamonds; two hearts — "bum steer" might be a spade and a club)

➼ cards sharing the same number (two 4s; two 7s; two 9s — "bum steer" might be a 4 and a 5)

➼ doubles (an Ace and a 2; a 2 and a 4; a 3 and a 6 — "bum steer" might be a 4 and a 7)

➼ same color suit (a diamond and a heart; a club and a spade; two spades — "bum steer" might be a club and a heart). This is a tough one!

➼ evens or odds (a 2 and a 10; a 3 and a 7; a 4 and an 8 — "bum steer" might be a 4 and a 7)

➼ triples (an Ace and a 3; a 2 and a 6; a 3 and a 9 — "bum steer" might be a 3 and a 10)

➼ same suit two apart (a 4 and a 6 of clubs; a 2 and a 4 of hearts; a 5 and a 7 of spades — "bum steer" could be either same suit but not two apart: e.g. 3 and 4 of diamonds; or two apart but not same suit: 5 of hearts and 7 of diamonds)

As you can see, using two attributes increases the difficulty level of the game considerably.

The Bum Steer
Sample Games Layout Master

Game A Sample Layout

Buckaroo Bob puts three steer in the corral, to see if Cowboy Casey can find another steer that belongs ...

... Cowboy Casey responds by choosing a steer from the deck and presenting it to Buckaroo Bob, who will let him know whether or not it belongs in the corral ...

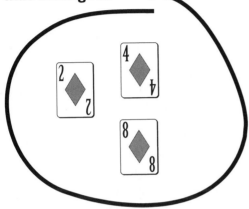

(Here the common attribute is "diamonds with even numbers.")

Yes, the 6 of diamonds does belong. One for Cowboy Casey!

Game B Sample Layout

Buckaroo Bob puts four steer in the corral, one of which doesn't belong, just to play a trick on Cowboy Casey.

Cowboy Casey looks at the four steer and tells Buckaroo Bob which one doesn't belong. If Casey is right, he gets to lead the "bum steer" out of the corral.

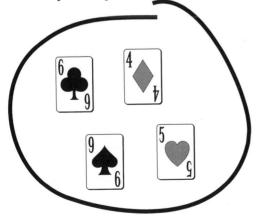

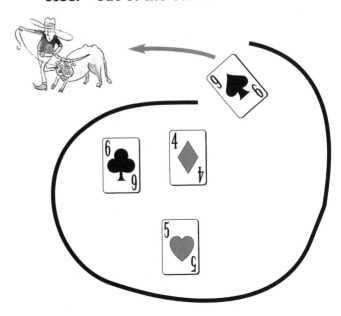

(Here the common attribute is "cards in the range of 4 to 6," so the 9 is the "bum steer.")

STORYLINE

Rival ranchers have arrived at the open range, and each wants to grab as much land as possible. To decide which Rancher will get which pieces of land, they set up a system. As long as just one of them claims a parcel, he gets to keep it. But any time they both claim the same piece of land, they are forced to give it to the cows. And any parcel that neither claims gets dedicated as Park Land.

CONCEPT CORRAL

ALGEBRA

➤ Use attributes of number, suit, and color to define groups of cards.

➤ Sort cards into sections of a Venn diagram.

REASONING

➤ Identify cards that have one of two attributes, that share two attributes, and that have neither of two attributes.

➤ Predict how many cards will belong to one group, to another group, both groups, and neither group.

Land Grab

GAME A Competitive

GOAL: For the Ranchers, the Cow, and the Park Ranger, to try to get the most acres of land. And later, to accurately predict how many acres of land each will get.

 # Players: 3, or 4.

1 Children at each group assign themselves roles. With three children, one is Rancher #1, second is Rancher #2, third child is the Cow. With four children, add a role for Park Ranger. This child takes all acres (cards) that get discarded. The idea is that these acres get preserved as Park Land.

2 Educator gives children a "split-rule" by which they decide how the players divide up the land. Split-rule example we'll use in this write-up: Rancher #1 gets all acres (cards) marked with black suits; Rancher #2 gets all acres with even numbers; Cow therefore gets all acres marked with both black suits and even numbers. That is, Cow gets overlap area on Venn Diagram. Park Ranger gets all acres that are neither black nor even — the cards that are red and odd. (See Tips & Pointers #1 and 2 for more split-rule ideas.)

3 Each child writes his aspect of split-rule in space provided on Land Grab Gameboard, copied off master on p.53. e.g. Rancher #1 writes, "black"; Rancher #2 writes, "even"; Cow writes, "black and even"; Park Ranger writes, "red and odd."

4 Children shuffle deck, turn cards face down, and turn over first card. If it falls in category of Rancher #1, Rancher #1 says, "Mine!" and places card on Gameboard's Rancher #1 space. If it falls in category of Rancher #2, Rancher #2 says, "Mine!" and places it on Rancher #2 space. If both Ranchers say "Mine," Cow says "Moo!" and places card on the overlap Cow space. If neither Rancher claims card, Park Ranger says, "Open Space" and puts card on Gameboard's Open Space area. Here's an example with our split-rule. If card is 3 of clubs, Rancher #1 gets it since the card, being a club, is black. If card is 4 of diamonds, Rancher #2 gets it since card's number (4) is even. If card is 6 of spades, Cow gets it since card is both black and even. If card is 5 of hearts, neither Rancher claims it, therefore Park Ranger gets it.

5 Children run through all 40 cards in deck. When finished, they count up how many acres each won, and they write these numbers on the "Actual #" line on Gameboard.

6 After children have played the game this way a few times, educator asks children to predict how many cards each child will get. They write down their predictions on the "Prediction #" line for each character on Gameboard. Then have children play, and see if their predictions are close or correct. Once they have some experience making predictions, it's a good time to ask Campfire Chat Questions #1 through 6.

7 If your children have trouble making accurate predictions, go to Campfire Chat Question #7.

CAMPFIRE CHAT

*1 Is there any skill involved in getting the most acres? Or is this just a matter of luck? And if it is just a matter of luck, what kind of luck do you need to get the most acres? **A: No skill involved. Number of acres each child gets depends solely on the nature of the split-rule, and which role a child plays. i.e. The split-rule determines in advance how many cards each character will get. So the only luck involved is for a child to play the role that is predetermined to get the most cards.**

2 What strategies did you use to predict who will get the most acres? Was your strategy accurate? **A: Answers will vary, but responses will give educator clues as to how well children understand how the split-rule works.**

3 What would happen if split-rule states that Rancher #1 gets all even cards, while Rancher #2 gets all odd cards? Why would this make for a boring game? **A: If cards are split odd vs. even, Cow gets no cards, for there's no overlap.**

*4 Can you think of another split rule that would lead to the Cow getting no cards? **A: Here are two others. Rancher #1 gets black cards, while Rancher #2 gets red cards. Or Rancher #1 gets all cards Aces through 5s, while Rancher #2 gets all cards 6s through 10s.**

*5 Now can you make a split-rule that allows the Cow to get at least some cards? **A: As long as there is some overlap, Cow will get cards. One way to see this clearly is with split-rules using number intervals. Example: Rancher #1 gets Aces and 2s; Rancher #2 gets 2s and 3s. It's clear that the 2s are an overlap zone, and Cow will therefore get the 2s.**

*6 Suppose split rule states that Rancher #1 gets all spades, and Rancher #2 gets all 8s, 9s, and 10s. Can you predict exactly how many acres each character will get? **A: Yes, using what they now know, children should be able to see that Rancher #1 gets all spades except the 8, 9, and 10 of spades (which Cow gets), for a total of 7 acres. Rancher #2 gets all 8s, 9s, and 10s except the 8, 9, and 10 of spades (which Cow gets) for a total of 9 acres. Cow gets three acres (the 8, 9, and 10 of spades, as stated above). And Park Ranger gets all remaining cards. Since there are 40 cards**

ROUNDUP

FOR EACH GROUP OF CHILDREN:

➤ Deck with all cards except picture cards and Jokers.

➤ One copy of the Land Grab Gameboard, copied off master on p.53.

in deck, subtract as follows: 40 – (7 + 9 + 3) = 21 acres for Park Ranger.

7 Is there a general procedure for predicting how many cards each will get? **A: Yes. First figure out how many each Rancher would get if no cards are shared. Then subtract number Cow gets from number of each Rancher. Finally, subtract Ranchers' and Cow's acres from the 40 in deck to get number that Park Ranger gets. Another example: Split-rule states that Rancher #1 gets all hearts, while Rancher #2 gets 5s and 10s. If there were no sharing, Rancher #1 would get 10 acres (since there are 10 hearts); Rancher #2 would get 8 acres (since there are four 5s and four 10s); Cow would get two acres (5 of hearts and 10 of hearts). To get Ranchers' true amounts, subtract Cow's two acres from each Rancher's total. True totals are therefore: Rancher #1, 8 acres (10 – 2); Rancher #2, 6 acres (8 – 2); and Cow, 2. Since that's a total of 16 acres, Park Ranger gets 24 acres, since 40 – 16 = 24.**

*8 Can you think of any situations in everyday life where there's a split-rule that breaks things into four, Venn-diagram-like groups? **A: Answers will vary, but here are two examples to trigger ideas. a) Children with blond hair / children with blue eyes / children with blond hair and blue eyes / children with neither blond hair nor blue eyes. b) Children who have cats / children who have dogs / children with cats and dogs / children with neither cats nor dogs. (Follow-up: create life-size Venn diagrams with children breaking into such groups.)**

TIPS AND POINTERS

1 Here are a few suggested split-rules for starting out:
↠ Rancher #1 gets all black cards; Rancher #2 gets all even cards.
↠ Rancher #1 gets all red cards; Rancher #2 gets all odd cards.
↠ Rancher #1 gets all spades; Rancher #2 gets all cards from 8s through 10s.
↠ Rancher #1 gets all hearts; Rancher #2 gets all multiples of 5 (5s and 10s).
↠ Rancher #1 gets all cards Aces through 4s; Rancher #2 gets all cards 3s through 6s.
↠ Rancher #1 gets all cards 3s through 7s; Rancher #2 gets all cards 5s through 9s.
↠ Rancher #1 gets all spades and diamonds; Rancher #2 gets all even cards.
↠ Rancher #1 gets all even black cards; Rancher #2 gets all spades.
↠ Rancher #1 gets all cards with ages of herself and her siblings (e.g. 4s, 7s, 9s); Rancher #2 gets all red cards.

2 Here is a list of attributes educator (or children) can use in various combinations to create original split-rules:
↠ black (or red) cards (clubs and spades; hearts and diamonds).
↠ cards of a certain suit (clubs, spades, hearts, or diamonds).
↠ cards of two suits but not the same color suit (spades and hearts, spades and diamonds, clubs and hearts, clubs and diamonds).
↠ cards wtih even numbers (2s, 4s, 6s, 8s, 10s).
↠ cards with odd numbers (Aces, 3s, 5s, 7s, 9s).
↠ cards below a certain number (e.g. 4s and less: 4s, 3s, 2s, and Aces).
↠ cards above a certain number (e.g. 8s and above: 8s, 9s, 10s).
↠ cards in a certain interval (e.g. 4s through 7s: 4s, 5s, 6s, and 7s).
↠ multiples of 5 (5s and 10s).
↠ multiples of 3 (3s, 6s, and 9s).
↠ factors of 10 (Aces, 2s, 5s, and 10s).
↠ factors of 12 (Aces, 2s, 3s, 4s, and 6s).

3 Laminate and use dry-erase marker on the playing mat so that children can easily erase between games.

Rancher #1

I get all acres that are ...

Prediction #: _____

Actual #: _____

Cow

I get all acres that are ...

Prediction #: _____

Actual #: _____

Rancher #2

I get all acres that are ...

Prediction #: _____

Actual #: _____

Park Ranger

I get all acres that are ...

Prediction #: _____

Actual #: _____

"High Five!"

GOAL: Buckaroos work together to figure out the relative values of the cards in their hands. If they succeed, they become partners for the upcoming roundup.

 # Players: 2.

STORYLINE

Buckaroos search for partners to help them round up cattle. Since working a roundup requires that two cowpokes think as one, each buckaroo must find a partner who thinks like her. To find the right partner, buckaroos play a game of high concentration. In this game, children give each other a "High Five!" every time the two of them think as one. If two cowpokes do well at this game, it means they're perfect partners.

CONCEPT CORRAL

NUMBER & OPERATION
➤ Use concepts of greater than, less than, and equal to, to compare both numbers and sums of numbers.

DATA ANALYSIS & PROBABILITY
➤ Determine likelihood that one's hand is greater than, less than, or equal to value of partner's hand.

REASONING
➤ Use process of elimination (POE) to figure out which cards are left, based on which cards have been played.

54

1 Dealer creates deck (see Roundup for Game A), shuffles, and deals herself and her partner one face-down card.

2 Each player picks up her card (not showing it to partner) and tries to determine if her card's number is higher or lower than number on partner's card.

3 On this first round, non-dealer guesses first, stating whether she thinks her card's number is greater than, less than, or equal to partner's card. Then partner, based on number on her card and what other player has said, states whether she thinks her card is greater than, less than, or equal to her partner's card.

4 Then the two partners lay down their cards. If neither made a correct guess, they leave the Round 1 box on Scoring Sheet empty. If either child made a correct guess, they make one check in Round 1 box. If both made correct guesses, they give each other a "High Five!" and make two checks in Round 1 box. After first round, children lay the cards just played face up in a space where both can easily see them (see Sample Games Layout sheet on p.58).

5 Dealer again deals two more cards: one for herself, one for partner. This time dealer guesses first. If children both guess correctly, they give each other a "High Five!" They again record the number of correct guesses with check marks in Round 2 scoring box. Once again, children lay down and organize cards played in an easily viewed space.

6 On third round, non-dealer guesses first. Now each child tries to figure out the exact card that the other child holds — by looking at cards played and using process of elimination (POE). See Campfire Chat #5. To get a check on this final round, each child must state exact value of partner's card. e.g. One child might say, "You have a 3," while the other says, "And you have an Ace." If both children figure out value of each other's cards, they give each other a "High Five!" and make two checks in the Round 3 scoring space. If only one child figures out value of partner's card, they make just one check.

7 Children add up the total number of checks for the three rounds and record that number in the Subtotal Box on Scoring Sheet.

8 Children play the game three times, for a total of 9 rounds. Children then record their Grand Total by adding up their three subtotals. The highest possible subtotal is 6, so highest Grand Total is 18. The partnership rankings are as follows: 18 = Perfect Partners; 15 to 17 = Dandy Partners; 14 to 15 = So-So Partners; 13 or less = Mismatched Partners.

GOAL: Buckaroos work together to figure out the relative values of the sums of cards in their hands. If they succeed, they become partners for the upcoming roundup.

 # Players: 2.

Rules: Same as Game A, only now deck's size is doubled (See Roundup), and dealer gives each child two cards on each of the three rounds. On every round, children try to predict whether the SUM of their two cards is greater than, less than, or equal to SUM of partner's cards. And on Round 3, children must use process of elimination to figure out the exact SUM of partner's cards to earn check marks. Use same partnership rankings as in Game A.

GOAL: Buckaroos work together to figure out the relative values of cards in their hands. If they succeed, they become partners for the upcoming roundup.

 # Players: 2.

Rules: Same as Game A, only now deck also contains two 4s (see Roundup), and there are four rounds per game. Highest Grand Total in this game and in Game D is 24. So partnership rankings are as follows: 24 = Perfect Partners; 21 to 23 = Dandy Partners; 18 to 20 = So-So Partners; 19 or less = Mismatched Partners.

GOAL: Buckaroos work together to figure out the relative values of the sums of cards in their hands. If they succeed, they become partners for the upcoming roundup.

 # Players: 2.

Rules: Same as Game B, only now deck also contains four 4s (see Roundup), and there are four rounds per game. As in Game B, children must use process of elimination in Round 4 to figure out the exact SUM of their partner's cards, in order to get check marks. Use same partnership rankings as in Game C.

ROUNDUP

FOR EACH PAIR OF CHILDREN:

➼ **Game A:** Deck with two Aces, two 2s, two 3s. One "High Five!" Game A / B Scoring Sheet, copied off master on p.59.

➼ **Game B:** Deck with four Aces, four 2s, four 3s. One "High Five!" Game A / B Scoring Sheet, copied off master on p.59.

➼ **Game C:** Deck with two Aces, two 2s, two 3s, two 4s. One "High Five!" Game C / D Scoring Sheet, copied off master on p.59.

➼ **Game D:** Deck with four Aces, four 2s, four 3s, four 4s. One "High Five!" Game C / D Scoring Sheet, copied off master on p.59.

➼ **Sample Games Layout** sheet, copied off master on p.58.

1 Why CAN YOU NEVER BE SURE on Round 1 whether or not your guess is correct? **A: On Round 1 you can never be sure because not enough cards have been played to let you be sure. Example for Game A: Suppose you get an Ace on Round 1. You might think your card is less than partner's card, but it's possible that partner also has an Ace. So you cannot be sure that card you hold is less. Example for Game D: Suppose you get two 4s on Round 1. You might think your SUM, 8, is greater than partner's SUM, but it's possible — while unlikely — that partner also has two 4s. So you cannot be certain that your SUM is greater.**

2 Are there situations in Round 2 in which you CAN BE SURE that your guess is correct? **A: Yes. Example for Game A: Suppose that on Round 1 the cards played are an Ace and a 2. On Round 2 you get an Ace. Since there are only two Aces, and you hold the second Ace, your partner cannot have an Ace. Therefore your partner must have a card greater than an Ace (a 2 or a 3). Therefore you can be certain that your Ace is less than partner's card. Example for Game D: Suppose that on Round 1 the cards played are one 3 and three 4s. On Round 2, you get dealt a 4 and a 3, for a sum of 7. You know your partner cannot have a 4, since your 4 is the only 4 left. Therefore, even if your partner has the greatest possible sum (6 = two 3s), you still have the greater sum. So you can be confident in saying that your hand has a greater SUM.**

3 Are there situations in Round 2 in which you CANNOT BE SURE whether or not your guess is correct? **A: Yes, there are many Round 2 situations in which you cannot be sure that your guess is correct. Example for Game A: Suppose that on Round 1 cards played are an Ace and a 3. On Round 2 you get a 2. There is no way for you to know if your 2 is greater than, less than, or equal to partner's card, for your partner could have an Ace, 2, or 3. Example for Game D: On Round 1 cards played are one Ace, one 2, one 3, and one 4. On Round 2, you are dealt a 2 and a 3, for a SUM of 5. There are so many possibilities left that your partner could easily have a SUM less than yours (e.g. two Aces), a SUM equal to yours (e.g. an Ace and a 4), or a SUM greater than yours (e.g. two 4s).**

4 Are there situations in Round 2 in which studying the cards played can help you make a better guess? **A: Yes. Example for Game A: On Round 1 the cards played are an Ace and a 2. On Round 2, you get a 2. Using POE, you reason that the three cards left (one held by your partner, the other two not yet played) must be one Ace and two 3s. This tells you two things. First, you should not guess "equal" for there's no way your partner can have a 2.**

Secondly, it's more likely that partner has a 3 than an Ace, for there are two 3s left, but only one Ace left. By reasoning this out, your best guess is to say that your 2 is less than partner's card, for she most likely has a 3.

* 5 How can you figure out exactly what card(s) partner has on the final round. **A: You can figure out your partner's card(s) by using POE. Example for Game A: After Round 2, the cards that have been played are the two Aces, one 2, and one 3. Using POE, you know that the two cards left are a 2 and a 3. If you are dealt the 2, partner has the 3, and vice-versa. Example for Game D: After Round 3, the cards played are the four Aces, three 2s, three 3s, and two 4s. Using POE, you reason that the cards left are one 2, one 3, and two 4s. If you are dealt a 2 and a 4, it means partner must have a 3 and a 4.**

* 6 Can you think of situations from life in which you might want to use POE? **A: To make this a journal entry question, it helps first to have some group discussion. If children seem stumped at first, educator may want to mention a few situations. Examples: a) Detectives use POE. If they know that one of three people must have committed a crime, and they rule out two of the three suspects, then the culprit must be the third suspect. b) Child trying to figure out what present she'll get on her birthday. If she asks for any of four presents, and she finds out she didn't get three of them, she must be getting the fourth one.**

TIPS AND POINTERS

1 When children lay down the cards that have been played, have them lay them out so that all cards of the same number are together and spread out, so all can be seen at one time. i.e. They should make a column of Aces, a column of 2s, a column of 3s, etc. See Sample Games Layout sheet on p.58 for examples.

2 It's good to model the situations described in Campfire Chat #1 – 5 if you want to have children learn to use POE to maximum benefit.

"High Five!"
Sample Games Layout Master

Game A — Round 3

**In your hand,
you hold ...**

Using **POE**, you reason that
partner must have a 2.
So you say your hand is
GREATER than hers.

Cards played ...

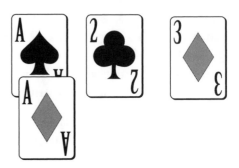

Game D — Round 4

**In your hand,
you hold ...**

Using **POE**, you reason that partner
must have a 3 and a 2.
So you say that your hand is
LESS than hers.

Cards played ...

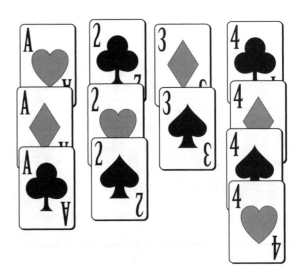

"High Five!"
Scoring Sheet Master

Game A / B Scoring Sheet

Round 1	Round 2	Round 3	Subtotal

Grand Total:

- -

Game C / D Scoring Sheet

Round 1	Round 2	Round 3	Round 4	Subtotal

Grand Total:

The rodeo's in town, and young buckaroos compete at the Bucking Bronco event. To do so, they must figure out an input-output rule, that is, the rule for a function. If the Bronco bucks them three times before they figure out the rule, they get knocked to the ground. But if they figure out the rule before getting knocked off, they win a Rodeo Trophy.

CONCEPT CORRAL

NUMBER & OPERATION
➻ Keeping score, which involves counting by 3s and 5s, and using subtraction (in Game B).

ALGEBRA
➻ Create, name, and identify function rules.

DATA ANALYSIS
➻ Use data from guesses to figure out the nature of a function.

REASONING
➻ Use information from two kinds of guesses to figure out nature of a function.

Bucking Bronco

GAME A
Cooperative/Competitive

GOAL: For Creating Team — to make and use an input-output rule.
For Guessing Team — to figure out the input-output rule before the Bucking Bronco knocks them to the dirt.

 # Players: 2, or 4. With 2, play one vs. one; with 4, play pair vs. pair.

1 Children in each group split into two teams: a Creating Team, which makes an input-output rule; and a Guessing Team, which tries to guess the rule.

2 Children spread entire deck on floor or tabletop and turn all cards face up.

3 Children on Creating Team confer and secretly make an input-output rule. e.g. Rule might be: Add 2 to any card presented. Creating Team writes its rule on a sheet of paper and hides it till the end of the round.

4 Guessing Team picks any card from all cards and places it face up on leftmost "INPUT" space on Bucking Bronco Card Mat.

5a Creating Team responds by following input-output rule it wrote down. Example: Suppose rule is ADD 2, and Guessing Team presents a 5 of hearts as "INPUT." Following its ADD 2 rule, Creating Team returns a 7 by placing it on the "OUTPUT" space on Card Mat, just below the 5 of hearts. (In this example, suit plays no role; i.e. Given 5 of hearts, Creating Team may return a 7 of any suit.) Guessing Team studies the two cards, the 5 and 7, trying to figure out the input-output rule.

5b In some cases, no card may be returned, and this is a key part of the fun. Example: Suppose that with rule ADD 2, Guessing Team presents a 10. Since there's no 12 card, no card may be returned. In such a case, Creating Team places a Bucking Bronco #1 Card, copied off master on p.64, on the "OUTPUT" space below the 10.

6 If Guessing Team presents a second card that merits a Bucking Bronco card, Creating Team places Bucking Bronco #2 Card on appropriate "OUTPUT" space. If Guessing Team present a third card that merits a Bucking Bronco card, Creating Team places Bucking Bronco #3 Card on appropriate "OUTPUT" space, and Creating Team reveals its rule. Then teams switch roles, and a new round begins.

7 Whenever Guessing Team thinks it knows rule, it tells Creating Team. If Guessing Team is right, teams switch roles, and a new round begins. If Guessing Team is wrong, play resumes. Guessing Team is allowed one guess for every input-output pair of cards laid down.

GOAL: For Creating Team — to make and use an input-output rule.
For Guessing Team — to figure out the input-output rule before the Bucking Bronco knocks them to the dirt.

 # Players: 2, or 4. With 2, play one vs. one; with 4, play pair vs. pair.

1 Play is the same as in Game A, but now teams keep score.

2 Guessing Team gets 5 points for correctly identifying the rule, but loses one point for each Bucking Bronco card it receives. Example: If Guessing Team correctly guesses rule after receiving two Bucking Bronco cards, it receives a total of 3 points (5 for guessing the rule minus 2 for the two Bucking Bronco cards).

3 If Creating team stumps Guessing Team by giving them three Bucking Bronco cards, Creating Team earns 3 points.

4 Educator or teams can decide how many points it takes to win. Or, play so that after a certain number of rounds, higher-scoring team wins.

CAMPFIRE CHAT

1 Were there any rules that the Guessing Team was able to figure out easily? If so, which ones? **A: Answers will vary. But often children find that simple ADD 1, ADD 2, SUBTRACT 1, SUBTRACT 2 rules are easiest to figure out.**

2 Were there any rules that the Guessing Team found difficult to figure out? If so, which ones? **A: Answers will vary. But usually children find that rules become harder to guess as the number of attributes involved increases. (See Tips & Pointers #3 for examples of functions with varying numbers of attributes.)**

3 Did your group ever get into an argument, with Creating Team insisting that its rule was valid, while the Guessing Team thought it was unfair? If so, how did you resolve this argument? **A: Answers will vary, but this can lead to a discussion about what makes a rule fair.**

4 Did anyone at your group come up with any original function rules? If so, can you tell everyone what your rule was? **A: Answers will vary.**

* 5 Can you describe your favorite input-output rule and give examples showing how it works? **A: Answers will vary.**

* 6 What kinds of things in life work like the Bucking Bronco type rules? In other words, can you think of situations in life in which something goes in, and then as a result, something comes out (e.g. Put money in a vending machine, push button, and out comes the product)? To make this a journal entry, it's best to have a group discussion first.

ROUNDUP

FOR EACH PLAYER OR TEAM:

➼ One deck of all cards: Ace through 10, plus all picture cards. For advanced play, add Joker, and let it stand for zero.

➼ Bucking Bronco status cards, copied off master on p.64. You'll need to run this off so that each group has one of each of the three Bucking Bronco cards.

➼ Rodeo trophies, copied off master on p.65.

➼ Bucking Bronco Card Mat, three or four for each group, copied off master on p.63 A few of these sheets should be laid end to end, for a team may need to use several sheets in any round of play.

1 Educator may want to model game for group by choosing children to come up and present a card. Educator responds by giving child a card that meets function rule — or a Bucking Bronco (BB) card, if no card can be given back. Since whole group tries to figure out rule, this offers a non-intimidating way for children to get game concept.

2 When modeling game, let children see that getting Bucking Bronco (BB) cards is not entirely negative, for these cards provide useful info. e.g. Guessers present a 7 and get back a 2. Looks like rule may be ADD 2. Then guessers present a 9 and get a BB card. This adds weight to theory that rule is ADD 2, for it now appears that they got the BB card because there is no 11 card.

3 It's helpful to model examples from the lists below to stimulate children's thinking. Educator may also want to copy this page and give it to students to help them come up with plenty of function ideas. Note: "BB" means that children get a Bucking Bronco card.

a) Examples of ONE-ATTRIBUTE FUNCTIONS:
➡ Add a number (e.g. Add 2, so sample pairs are 2 – 4; 5 – 7; 9 – BB).
➡ Subtract a number (e.g. Subtract 3, so sample pairs are 8 – 5; 6 – 3; 2 – BB).
➡ Double the number (sample pairs: 2 – 4; 5 – 10; 7 – BB).
➡ Two cards that add up to a certain number (e.g. Add up to 7, so sample pairs are 4 – 3; 2 – 5; 9 – BB).
➡ Two cards whose difference is constant (e.g. Difference is 3, so sample pairs are 4 – 1; 6 – 9; 10 – 7, etc.).
➡ Keep the suit (sample pairs: 5 of hearts – Ace of hearts; 6 of clubs – 9 of clubs; Jack of diamonds – 5 of diamonds, etc.).
➡ Keep number or picture (sample pairs: 7 of diamonds – 7 of clubs; Queen of hearts – Queen of diamonds, etc.).
➡ ADVANCED: Black cards stand for positive numbers; red cards stand for negative numbers. Rule is add a number (e.g. Add -6, so sample pairs are black 2 – red 4; black Ace – red 5; black 9 – black 3; red 2 – red 8; etc.). This is a fun follow-up to studying positive and negative integers with "Steer on the Loose!" (pp.28–33)

b) Examples of TWO-ATTRIBUTE FUNCTIONS:
➡ Keep number, change suit color (2 of clubs – 2 of hearts; 8 of diamonds – 8 of spades).
➡ Add a number, keep suit (e.g. Add 4, so sample pairs are 3 of hearts – 7 of hearts; 2 of spades – 6 of spades; 7 of diamonds – BB).

c) Examples of THREE-ATTRIBUTE FUNCTIONS:
➡ Keep number, keep color, change suit (sample pairs: 2 of clubs – 2 of spades; 8 of diamonds – 8 of hearts).
➡ Subtract a number, keep color, change suit (e.g. Subtract 4, so sample pairs are 9 of clubs – 5 of spades; 5 of hearts – Ace of diamonds; 3 of clubs – BB).

4 Educator should state as overall rule that both Creating Team and Guessing Team must agree on how many attributes their functions will have at any given time.

Bucking Bronco Card Mat Master

Output

Input

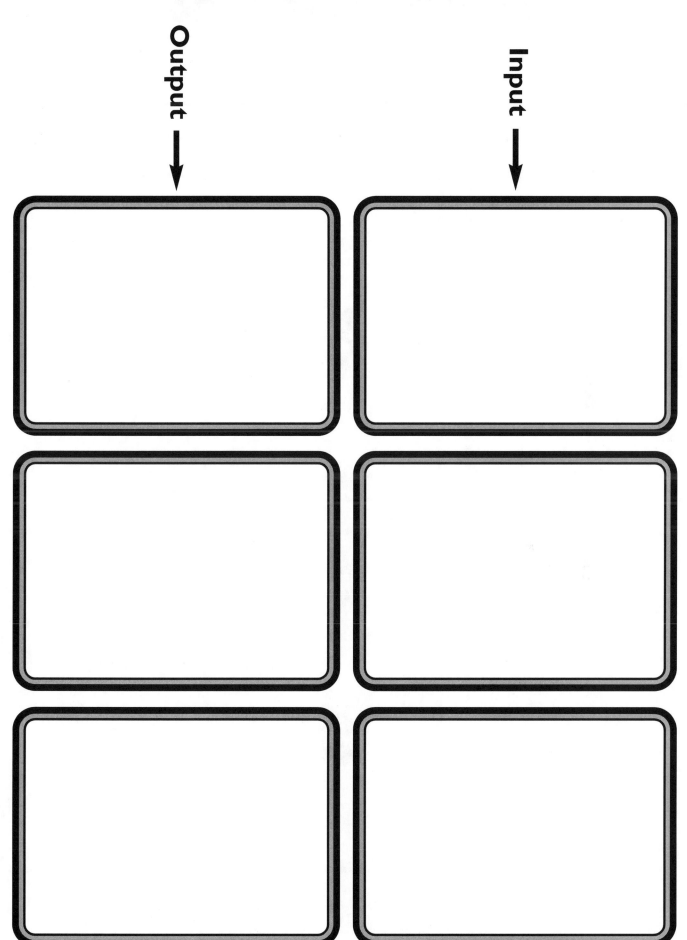

Bucking Bronco
Status Cards Master

Bucking Bronco #1

Bucking Bronco #2

Bucking Bronco #3

Bucking Bronco #1

Bucking Bronco #2

Bucking Bronco #3

Rodeo Trophy Master

Fix the Fence

After a big storm blows through, Rancher Katie notices that her fence has been badly damaged, with many fenceposts knocked down and scattered on the ground. Inspecting the fence, Katie remembers that there's a pattern to her fenceposts. To repair it, she needs to return the fenceposts to the right sequence. Help Katie put her fence back up before her cows escape!

CONCEPT CORRAL

NUMBER & OPERATION
➻ Create and recognize sequences involving numbers (ascending, descending, odd, even, etc.).

ALGEBRA
➻ Create and recognize sequences involving attributes (color and suits).

PROBLEM SOLVING & REASONING
➻ Find the missing element or elements in a sequence.

GOAL: To build a "fence" of cards that follows a sequence, and to conceal part of the sequence by turning over one card. Also, to give hints that help someone figure out the turned-over card.

GAME A Cooperative

 # Players: 1, 2, 3, or 4.

This is a good warm-up game for Games B and C.

1 Children first lay all cards in deck face up, and decide upon a sequence. Example: Children might decide to make a sequence that follows the pattern: red — red — black / red — red — black, etc. See Tips & Pointers #5 for the variety of sequences possible.

2 Children then lay out six cards in a row in a way that follows their sequence, placing all six cards face up. Then they turn any one of those six cards face down. See diagram on p.69. This row is called the "fence."

3 Educator comes along and tries to figure out a pattern in the fence of cards. i.e. Educator tries to figure out the rule behind the sequence.

4 Educator touches the face-down card and states what s/he thinks it is. For example, educator might say: "It's red," or "It's a club," or "It's a 5," or "It's the 9 of diamonds."

5a If educator is correct, children turn over the card.

5b If educator is wrong, children give educator a hint. In our example, children might say, "Think of groups of three," since their sequence is based on units of three, the pattern: red — red — black.

6 Educator gets two guesses. If educator cannot guess the card after two guesses, children show educator the card and explain their sequence.

7 Educator goes on to another group while children at first group make a new sequence.

8 Play continues in this fashion.

Variation: For more challenging play, have children lay out a total of five cards, or even just four cards, not six. This variation is a more difficult game because there are fewer face-up cards to clue the educator in to the nature of the sequence.

GOAL: Using cards, to make a sequence that is challenging for other children to figure out. Also, to offer hints that help children figure out the sequence.

 # Players: 2, or 4.

1 Each group creates a "fence" (row) of six cards within parameters set by educator (e.g. "Fence sequences are based on number only." Or "Fence sequences are based on number and suit.") See Tips & Pointers #5. Each group then turns one of its six cards face down.

2 Each group then splits up into a set of Fence Fixers and Fence Checkers. With 2, split up 1 and 1; with 4, split up pair and pair.

3 While Fence Checkers stay at the table, Fence Fixers mosey over to another group to try to repair their fence.

4 At each table, Fence Fixers study the fence sequence and the missing fencepost (face-down card), and make a guess as to what the face-down card is. e.g. Fence Fixers might say, "The missing fencepost is the 3 of spades."

5a If Fence Fixers are right, Fence Checkers give Fence Fixers one token. Then Fence Fixers go to another group and try to fix their fence. Note: Tell Fence Checkers to leave their face-down card face down for the next Fence Fixers.

5b If Fence Fixers' guess is wrong, Fence Checkers tell them so but do not turn over the card. Fence Checkers then offer a hint to help the Fence Fixers figure out the missing fencepost. e.g. If the pattern involves odd numbers, Fence Checkers might say, "Think about odd and even numbers."

6 Fence Fixers get three guesses to figure out the broken fencepost. If they do not guess it in three tries, Fence Checkers show them the card. Then Fence Fixers go to another group and try to repair their fence.

GOAL: To make patterns that other students have trouble figuring out.

 # Players: 2, or 4.

Same basic rules as Game B. The only difference is that now the Fence Checkers do not offer hints if the Fence Fixers make incorrect guesses. And Fence Fixers get only two tries to guess the face-down card, the "broken fencepost." Whichever group of Fence Fixers repairs three fences first wins the game.

ROUNDUP

FOR EVERY GROUP OF PLAYERS:

➥ Deck with all cards except picture cards and Jokers.

➥ OPTIONAL: Two such decks, to let children build longer fence sequences, or fences that require cards from more than one deck (e.g. a fence that requires two 6 of diamonds or three black 7s).

➥ Games B and C only: Tokens that let Fence Fixers keep track of the number of fences they fix. Use any small object, like buttons, play money, etc.

➥ OPTIONAL: Sample Game Layout on bottom of p.69, to give children a sense of how the game is played.

*1 What difficulties did you face while trying to build your fence? And did you ever disagree about which card you should turn over? **A:** **Answers will vary.**

*2 For the Fence Fixers, what strategies did you use to figure out the sequence? **A:** **Answers will vary.**

3 Did the Fence Fixers and Fence Checkers ever get into any argument as to whether or not the sequence was valid? If so, how did you resolve your disagreement? **A:** **Answers will vary.**

TIPS AND POINTERS

1 Before play, it helps to demonstrate some sequences for children on an overhead, chalkboard, or tabletop.

2 Educator moderates level of difficulty by adjusting the kinds of sequences children are allowed to create (See Tips & Pointer #5). It's good to start out with the easier sequences and progress gradually toward more difficult ones.

3 While games as described suggest children lay out six cards and turn one face down, educator can also moderate ease or difficulty of play by varying these numbers. Example: For easier play, have children lay out more cards. For harder play, have children turn more cards face down. Educator can also increase both numbers and keep play at the same level of difficulty. Example: Lay out 12 cards and turn two of them face down. Feel free to experiment with different combinations of these numbers.

4 Point out that in some sequences there will be considerable freedom as to which card comes next, while in other patterns there is less freedom, or only one card that will extend the pattern. Examples: In the pattern: black — red / black — red, any black card extends the pattern. But in this pattern: Ace of spades — 2 of spades — 3 of spades — 4 of spades — 5 of spades, there is just one card, the 6 of spades, that extends the pattern.

5 EXAMPLES OF SEQUENCES (in increasing order of difficulty):

FOCUS ON COLOR (i.e. IGNORE number and suit):
➺ repeating in groups of two (red — black / red — black, etc.)
➺ repeating in groups of four (black — black — black — red / black — black — black — red, etc.)

FOCUS ON SUITS (i.e. IGNORE number and color):
➺ two alternating suits (diamond — club / diamond — club, etc.)
➺ three alternating suits (heart — diamond — club / heart — diamond — club, etc.)
➺ back & forth pattern (heart — diamond — club — diamond — heart — diamond — club, etc.)

FOCUS ON NUMBER (i.e. IGNORE suit and color):

➟ 2-card up-down sequence (5 — 6 — 5 — 6 — 5 — 6, etc.)

➟ 3-card ascending & repeating (Ace — 2 — 3 / Ace — 2 — 3, etc.)

➟ 3-card descending & repeating (10 — 9 — 8 / 10 — 9 — 8, etc.)

➟ ascending & descending (Ace — 2 — 3 — 4 — 5 — 4 — 3 — 2 — Ace — 2 — 3 — 4 — 5, etc.)

➟ evens ascending (2 — 4 — 6 — 8 — 10 / 2 — 4 — 6 — 8 — 10, etc.)

➟ odds ascending & descending: (Ace — 3 — 5 — 7 — 9 — 7 — 5 — 3 — Ace, etc.)

FOCUS ON COLOR AND NUMBER (i.e. IGNORE suits):

➟ ascending numbers, alternating colors (black 2 — red 3 — black 4 — red 5 — black 6 — red 7, etc.)

➟ ascending & descending evens, alternating colors (red 2 — black 4 — red 6 — black 8 — red 10 — black 8 — red 6 — black 4, etc.)

➟ descending numbers, colors changing in a 2-then-1 pattern (black 10 — black 9 — red 8 — black 7 — black 6 — red 5, etc.). This is challenging!

FOCUS ON NUMBER AND SUIT (i.e. IGNORE color):

➟ descending numbers, alternating suits (10 of hearts — 9 of clubs — 8 of hearts — 7 of clubs — 6 of hearts — 5 of clubs, etc.)

➟ ascending numbers, suits changing after every round (Ace of spades — 2 of spades — 3 of spades — Ace of clubs — 2 of clubs — 3 of clubs — Ace of diamonds — 2 of diamonds, etc.)

➟ ascending & descending evens, alternating suits (2 of diamonds — 4 of spades — 6 of hearts — 8 of clubs — 10 of diamonds — 8 of spades — 6 of hearts — 4 of clubs, etc.)

FIX THE FENCE
SAMPLE GAME LAYOUT

   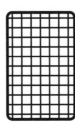  

(Missing card is the 5 of clubs, for sequence involves increases by one, and alternating hearts and clubs.)

STORYLINE

Mysterious Bandits are on the loose, robbing money from banks, trains, and innocent frontier people. Young buckaroos get deputized and try to capture these dastardly Bandits. To do so, they need to figure out the missing number in addition and subtraction problems. Each number they figure out means that another member of the Mysterious Bandit gang is locked away.

CONCEPT CORRAL

NUMBER & OPERATION
➤ Add and subtract whole numbers.

ALGEBRA
➤ Figure out the value of a missing number.

PROBLEM SOLVING
➤ Develop strategies for discovering the value of a variable.

REASONING
➤ Explain how to discover the value of a variable.
➤ Learn and apply strategies to see whether or not a problem involves regrouping.

CONNECTIONS
➤ Discover and describe links between addition and subtraction.

70

Mysterious Bandits

GAME A Competitive

GOAL: To nab Mysterious Bandits by discovering their value.

 # Players: 2, or 4. With 4, it's best to play pair vs. pair.

1 Educator sets a goal for how many Bandit Badges children must collect to win. Educator also tells children which worksheet to use (addition or subtraction) and tells them a two-digit number to write in at the bottom of the worksheet as the answer. Example: Using addition worksheet, educator might tell children to write **78** as answer. One child on each team writes this number as answer, at bottom of worksheet.

2 Children at each team break into two groups: Outlaws and Sheriffs. Sheriffs look away while Outlaws create a problem with designated number (**78**, in this example) as answer. e.g. **42 + 36 = 78**. Then Outlaws find and lay down two cards of first addend FACE UP on worksheet's top two spaces (in this case, a 4 and a 2, for 42). Outlaws also find two cards for second addend, and lay them FACE DOWN on worksheet's two middle spaces (in this case, a 3 and a 6, for 36). These two FACE-DOWN cards are the Bandits, which Sheriffs will try to "smoke out."

3 Outlaws present worksheet and cards to Sheriffs.

4 Sheriffs study the problem and try to determine value of FACE-DOWN cards. When they think they know, they state their value, then turn those cards over.

5a If guesses are right, Sheriffs get one Mysterious Bandit Badge, copied off master on p.75. Then teams switch roles, and play resumes.

5b If Sheriffs' guesses are wrong, teams switch roles, and play resumes.

6 Players win when they get as many badges as educator specifies it takes to win. Five is a good starting-out number. Increase it over time.

CAMPFIRE CHAT

*1 When using ADDITION Worksheet with Bandits in MIDDLE of worksheet, how did you figure out their value? **A: Answers will vary, but some children will describe the "adding up" process. e.g. In a situation like 3 + Bandit = 8, they say, "Since the top number was 3, and the answer number was 8, I just counted up 5 to get to 8, so the middle number had to be 5." Other children might**

describe a subtraction process, saying: "I knew that 8 – 3 is 5, so I knew the Bandit had to be 5." Such a response can stimulate discussion about connections between addition and subtraction.

*2 When using ADDITION Worksheet with Bandits at TOP of worksheet, how did you figure out Bandits' value? **A: Answers will vary, but some children will talk in terms of "adding up," as described above. Others may use language of subtraction. In a situation like Bandit + 5 = 8, a child might say, "I knew that the Bandit plus 5 equals 8. So I did 8 – 5 = 3 to get it." This kind of response can also stimulate talk about addition-subtraction connections.**

*3 When using SUBTRACTION Worksheet with Bandits on MIDDLE line, how did you figure out their value? **A: Answers will vary, but in this case children often say they figured out how much they needed to subtract from top card to get the number in answer. In a situation like 8 – Bandit = 5, a child might say: "I just counted down from 8 till I got 5, and it took 3 to get there. So the Bandit had to be 3."**

*4 When using SUBTRACTION Worksheet with Bandits on TOP line, how did you figure out their value? **A: Answers will vary, but some children will use language of addition, saying, for example, in a case like Bandit – 3 = 5: "I knew that if you take 3 away from the bandit, you get 5. So the bandit is 3 more than 5. So it had to be 8." This kind of response can also stimulate discussion about addition-subtraction links.**

5 If the two Bandit cards form the number 22, is there any difference between those two 2s? Or do they have the same value? **A: Depending on the extent of their exposure to place value, children may or may not be baffled by this question. Children should recognize that the 2 in the tens place stands for 20, while the 2 in the ones place stands for 2. If children don't have this concept firmly in place, asking this question will let educator know it needs further development.**

*6 Can you tell by glancing at an ADDITION problem whether or not it involves REGROUPING? **A: Yes. If ANSWER DIGIT in ones PLACE is less than ADDEND DIGIT in ones PLACE, problem involves regrouping. Example: in 27 + Bandits = 43, ANSWER DIGIT in ones place is 3, while addend digit in ones place is 7. Since answer digit (3) is less than addend digit (7), problem involves regrouping.**

*7 Can you tell by glancing at a SUBTRACTION problem whether or not it involves REGROUPING? **A: Yes, and there are two methods**

ROUNDUP

FOR EACH GROUP OF CHILDREN:

➤ One deck with all 10s, and picture cards removed. Include Jokers, and have them stand for the number zero (0).

➤ Mysterious Bandit Worksheet A, copied off master on p.73, for the addition game; Mysterious Bandit Worksheet B, copied off master on p.74, for the subtraction game. Make one copy per team of whichever worksheet children use.

➤ A bowl or envelope filled with Mysterious Bandit Badges copied off master on p.75. Make sure each team has plenty of badges.

for checking this out — one for each possible set-up. **METHOD ONE:** used when Bandits are on **TOP** line — the 'minuend.' **ADD 1s DIGIT** in **ANSWER** to 1s **DIGIT** in **MIDDLE LINE**, the 'subtrahend.' If sum exceeds 9, problem involves regrouping. Example: Bandits − 15 = 19. ADD the 9 and the 5. Since their sum (14) exceeds 9, problem involves regrouping. Method Two: used when Bandits are on middle line — subtrahend. Check if ones **DIGIT** in top line (minuend) is less than ones **DIGIT** in **ANSWER**. If so, problem involves regrouping; if not, it does not involve regrouping. Example: 34 − Bandits = 19. Just compare the 4 with the 9. Since 4 is **LESS** than 9, problem involves regrouping.

TIPS AND POINTERS

1 If you have children still working on single-digit addition and subtraction, you can modify game by having children use just the ones place on worksheets.

2 Variations that lead to more challenging play:

a) Place FACE-UP cards on Gameboard's two middle spaces instead of on top two spaces, **b)** Use Subtraction Worksheet instead of Addition Worksheet, **c)** When using Subtraction Worksheet, place FACE-UP cards on Gameboard's two middle spaces instead of on top two spaces, **d)** When using either worksheet, allow children to create problems that require regrouping. e.g. 43 + 19 = 62, or 81 − 47 = 34. Introducing regrouping problems leads to a "quantum leap" in challenge and difficulty.

3 Once children have had ample practice using one number for the answer, educator may want to choose a new number for the answer, to keep things lively.

4 Here's a way to encourage independent work. Take a bunch of index cards, and write a two-digit number on each index card (e.g. 47, 93, 16, etc.). Create several stacks of 10 cards, and give one stack to each group's Outlaws. Outlaws pick a card off top of stack, and they have to use that number as the answer.

5 Using the format of Tips & Pointers #4 above, you can challenge students a bit more by letting them use the number drawn as any of the three lines of the problem. Example: If they draw a 47, they could use 47 as the top line, the middle line, or as the answer to the problem. Let children know that they may end up using numbers that go into the hundreds place. If that happens, children can move away from using the worksheets and just lay problems out on their desks.

6 For a high-level challenge, Outlaws arrange the two face-down cards so that they are diagonal to each other. Example: In a problem like 62 − 15 = 47, the two face-down cards could be either the 6 and the 5, or they could be the 2 and the 1. Sheriffs can solve for the face-down cards, but doing so requires more thought.

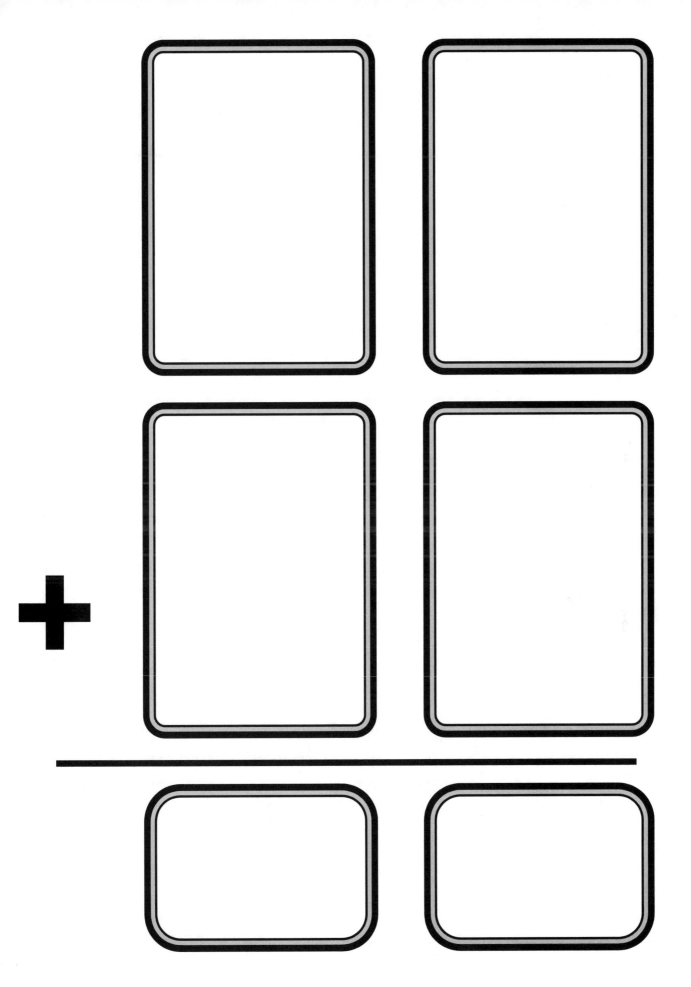

Mysterious Bandit Worksheet B Master — Subtraction

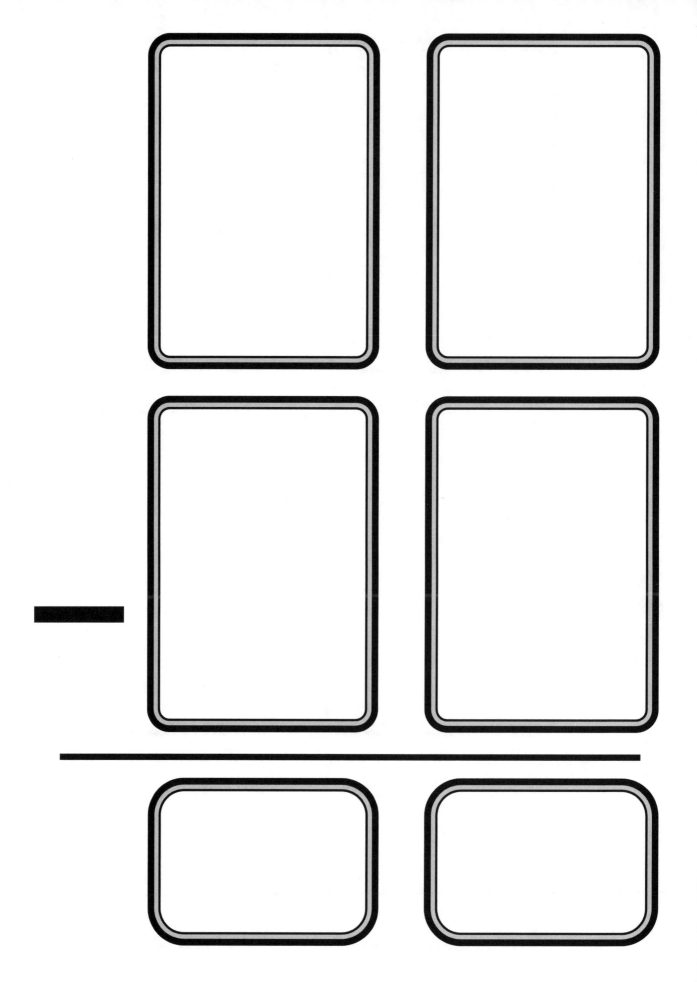

© 2003 by Singing Turtle Press

Bandit Badges Master

Found and Arrested

Marvin the Moustache

Found and Arrested

"Rowdy" Ramona

Found and Arrested

"Sweet-Tooth" Swen

Found and Arrested

"Holdup" Harriet

Found and Arrested

Cheatin' Charlie

Found and Arrested

"Pickpocket" Patty

Found and Arrested

Marvin the Moustache

Found and Arrested

"Rowdy" Ramona

Found and Arrested

"Sweet-Tooth" Swen

Found and Arrested

"Holdup" Harriet

Found and Arrested

Cheatin' Charlie

Found and Arrested

"Pickpocket" Patty

Cows in the Pen

Ranchhand Rita faces a challenge. Her boss gives her a certain amount of fencing and asks her to build a rectangular pen holding as many cows as possible. Rita knows there are many ways to build her rectangular pen. If she figures out how to build the pen that holds the most cows, the Ranch Boss gives her an award. Help Rita get the job done right!

CONCEPT CORRAL

NUMBER & OPERATION
➤ Learn that length times width equals area.

GEOMETRY
➤ Learn concepts of perimeter, length, width, and area.

➤ Given a fixed perimeter, alter length and width to maximize area.

➤ Discover that there are many rectangles with a given perimeter, each of which has different dimensions and a different area.

CONNECTIONS
➤ See connections between addition and perimeter; between multiplication and area.

GAME A Cooperative

GOAL: To make various rectangular pens with the same amount of fencing, then find the pen that holds the most cows.

 # Players: 1, 2, 3, or 4 (can be played in a solitary fashion — a fun activity for children who finish assignments early).

1 Children shuffle cards, place deck face down, then take top card off deck and turn it over.

2 Children look at upturned card and double its value to get the perimeter. e.g. If card is 4, the perimeter they work with is 8.

3 Children gather as many "fenceposts" (i.e. toothpicks — see Roundup) as indicated by perimeter. Then they create a rectangle using those toothpicks serving as the side of the rectangle. The rectangle formed is the "pen" for holding the cows. Note: If any children have trouble making a rectangle with nice neat lines and angles, create a helper grid, as described in last item of Roundup.

4 After children make first rectangle, ask them to place cow squares, copied off master on p.80, inside rectangle, to see how many fit inside. Then children record the perimeter, length, width, and area (number of cows) on their Cows in the Pen Recording Sheet, copied off master on p.81.

5 Next children construct another rectangular pen with the same number of fenceposts but with different dimensions. Note that children will be able to create more than one rectangle as long as the perimeter they are working with is 8 or greater. See Data Chart on next page for details on all possible pen dimensions and areas.

6 As long as children can make a second pen with same perimeter, they do so, then place cows inside new pen to see how many fit inside. Children then record the perimeter, length, width, and area for this pen.

7 Children keep constructing rectangular pens until they have made as many as possible for their given perimeter.

GAME B
Competitive

GOAL: To construct the pen that holds the most cows more quickly than any other group.

 # Players: 2, or 4. With 4, play pair vs. pair.

Same rules as Game A, only now children compete one vs. one, or pair vs. pair. Childen at each group draw a card from the deck, double it to get perimeter. Then the two teams try to build a pen with that perimeter and containing the most cows more quickly than opposing team.

VARIATION: Children triple the values of the cards they draw. That way, they can get perimeters ranging from 6 (3 x 2) through 30 (3 x 10). Or they can quadruple the values of the cards, thereby working with perimeters from 8 (4 x 2) through 40 (4 x 10).

● ●

Cows in the Pen Data Chart

Perimeter	Width by Length	Area
4	1 x 1	1
6	1 x 2	2
8	1 x 3	3
8	2 x 2	4
10	1 x 4	4
10	2 x 3	6
12	1 x 5	5
12	2 x 4	8
12	3 x 3	9
14	1 x 6	6
14	2 x 5	10
14	3 x 4	12
16	1 x 7	7
16	2 x 6	12
16	3 x 5	15
16	4 x 4	16
18	1 x 8	8
18	2 x 7	14
18	3 x 6	18
18	4 x 5	20
20	1 x 9	9
20	2 x 8	16
20	3 x 7	21
20	4 x 6	24
20	5 x 5	25

ROUNDUP

FOR EACH GROUP OF CHILDREN:

➻ Deck with all 2s – 10s.

➻ At least 20 standard toothpicks (2 5/8" long). These can be found at most supermarkets or drug stores.

➻ At least 25 cow squares, copied off master on p.80 and cut out.

➻ One copy of the Cows in the Pen Recording Sheet, copied off master on p.81.

➻ **OPTIONAL but RECOMMENDED:** To make it easier for children to lay out rectangles with toothpicks, create a helper grid by using Grid master on p.79. Here are the three steps for making the grid:

1) Copy the master onto legal-sized paper (8.5" x 14"), using a 130% ENLARGEMENT value. For easier copying, you can tear this page out at the perforation.

2) Put four such sheets of legal paper together at a common center (like the four U.S. states meeting at "Four Corners") to create a grid that is 9 units long by 5 units wide.

3) Line dots up and tape the four sheets together.

77

*1 Did you have any trouble figuring out how to make a different rectangle with the same number of toothpicks after you made your first rectangle? If so, how did you overcome the difficulty? **A: Answers will vary, but children should in time recognize that they can make different rectangles by altering the length and width.**

2 Were you surprised to see that rectangles with the same perimeter can have different areas? What is strange about this? **A: Answers will vary, but many children are usually surprised to learn this interesting fact about rectangles.**

*3 As you look over your Recording Sheet, do you notice any pattern as to what kinds of rectangles tend to have room for the most cows? For the fewest cows? **A: Children should eventually see that, given a fixed perimeter, the area increases as the length and width approach one another in value. Children should also see that whenever they can construct a square, the square will have room for more cows than any of the rectangles. Conversely, the narrowest rectangles have room for the fewest cows.**

TIPS AND POINTERS

1 If you choose not to make a grid (see final Roundup item), model how to make rectangles using toothpicks. It helps to tell children that the toothpicks must make an "L" shape at the corners, and that the sides of the rectangle must all be perfectly straight.

2 If you do make the grid, tape all seams down so that neither the toothpicks nor the cow squares slide between the seams.

3 If you make the grid, here's a fun and interesting way you can use it. Suppose that children are working with a perimeter of 12. They should make three rectangles, a 1 x 5, a 2 x 4, and a 3 x 3. Using the grid, they can display all three of these rectangles at once, with the cows inside. This provides children a way to see that varying the length and width does truly alter the area.

Cows in the Pen
Cow Master

Cows in the Pen
Recording Sheet

Number of Fenceposts (PERIMETER)	Dimensions of Rectangle (LENGTH by WIDTH)		Number of Cows in the Pen (AREA)
	length	width	
	length	width	
	length	width	
	length	width	
	length	width	
	length	width	
	length	width	
	length	width	

Horseshoes

STORYLINE

Lounging around after a day on the dusty trail, young cowhands toss around "number horseshoes," trying to hit a Target Number on the peg. Each time they hit a Target Number three times, they get a "ringer" and thereby earn a point.

CONCEPT CORRAL

NUMBER & OPERATION

➤➤ Explore the effect of adding, subtracting, and multiplying whole numbers.

➤➤ Develop and use strategies for whole number computation.

Pre-req skill: beginning skills in computation.

GAME A Cooperative

GOAL: To get "ringers" by making three number sentences that equal a Target Number from 1 to 20.

 # Players: 1, 2, 3, or 4.

1 Educator chooses a Target Number from 1 to 20. Children write this number on "Target Number" line inside a box on Target Number Worksheet, copied off master on p.88.

2 Children lay out all cards in deck and use both cards and operation symbols to create a number sentence equalling Target Number. See Sample Number Sentences master on p.85 for examples.

3 Encourage children to make a variety of number sentences equalling Target number. e.g. If Target number is **16: 12 + 2 + 2 = 16** or **18 − 4 + 2 = 16** or **2 x 10 − 4 = 16**. NOTE: To display a two-digit number like 12, students put an Ace on the left, and a 2 to its right.

4 Children record their number sentences on lines in box on Target Number Worksheet. If you wish, to add more fun, have children cut out mini-horseshoes on Horseshoe master on p.87 and place them on Horeshoe Gameboard. When they create their first number sentence for Target Number, they place their mini-horseshoe on the 1 space. When they create two sentences, they move their horseshoe to the 2 space. And if and when they create a third sentence, they move mini-horseshoe to the 3 space, indicating that they rang the horseshoe. Children record how many ringers they get in the Tally and Total spaces on Gameboard.

5 After everyone has had a chance to make number sentences, have children come up and show the number sentences they created.

GAME B Cooperative

GOAL: To get "ringers" by making three number sentences that equal a Target Number, but with certain restrictions.

 # Players: 2, 3, or 4.

Same rules as Game A, only now educator imposes restrictions for an additional challenge. Example: If Target Number is 12, educator might say students must create sentences that use multiplication once and addition once. Students would need to come up with sentences like:

$$2 x 3 + 6 = 12$$
$$4 x 2 + 4 = 12$$
$$2 x 5 + 2 = 12$$

Here are more examples of restrictions educator may wish to use:

➺ Use addition once and subtraction once.

➺ Use multiplication once and subtraction once.

➺ Use multiplication, addition, and subtraction once each.

➺ Use certain numbers in your number sentence. e.g. Use the number 7 in your number sentence, or use both 2 and 6 in your number sentence.

➺ Use a certain number as the first number in your number sentence. e.g. Suppose TARGET NUMBER IS 12, and restriction is: USE 3 FIRST. Children could then make sentences like:

$$3 \times 5 - 3 = 12$$
$$3 + 10 - 1 = 12$$
$$3 \times 2 + 6 = 12$$

GOAL: To make number sentences more quickly than an opposing team.

 # Players: 2, 3, or 4.

Same basic idea as in Game A or Game B, only now children play in teams and compete against a nearby team, or against all other teams in group. Educator first states Target Number (and restriction, if playing Game B version). Teams try to make a number sentence equalling Target Number before opposing teams. As soon as a team thinks it has a correct number sentence, it shouts: "Ringer!" Educator comes by to verify that the number sentence equals Target Number (and follows restriction, if playing with restrictions). If so, that team gets one "Ringer." Educator keeps score by giving each team that gets a "ringer" one mini-horseshoe, copied off master on p.87.

🔥 CAMPFIRE CHAT ➤

1 Do you find some numbers harder to make than others? If so, why do you suppose that is? **A: Answers will vary.**

*2 Did you find any patterns that made it easy to make the same number in different ways? If so, can you describe a pattern you used? **A: Answers will vary, but often children will discover patterns like: 2 + 6 = 8; 3 + 5 = 8; 4 + 4 = 8, which they might describe by saying, "The first number goes up and the second number goes down." Or like: 3 + 7 = 10 and 7 + 3 = 10, in which case they might say, "You can switch the numbers around, and you get the same answer."**

3 Do you find it easier to use the addition, subtraction or multiplication symbol? What is easier about this operation for you? **A: Answers will vary, but usually children find addition easiest, subtraction next easiest, and multiplication the hardest.**

FOR EACH PAIR OR GROUP:

➺ Deck with all picture cards removed. Ace stands for 1. If you wish, use Joker to stand for 0.

➺ Sample Number Sentences sheet, copied off master on p.85, allows children to see card layout examples for different games.

➺ Horseshoe Symbols, copied off master on p.86. Give each group plenty of operation signs and one equal sign.

➺ Target Number Worksheet, copied off master on p.88. One for each group.

➺ OPTIONAL: Horseshoe Gameboard, copied off master on p.89. Give one to each group if you want groups to chart their success on the board.

➺ OPTIONAL: Horseshoes copied off master on p.87. These let children track their success on Gameboard.

4 Is there any limit to the number of ways that a certain target number can be made? How can you prove this? **A:** **There is no limit, as long as there's no limit to the numbers that can be used to make it. For example, 18 can be made in all these ways: 24 – 6 = 18; 25 – 7 = 18; 26 – 8 = 18, etc.**

*5 Does playing this game show you anything about numbers that you hadn't known before? If so, what? **A:** **Answers will vary.**

TIPS AND POINTERS

1 When assigning Target Number, consider ability level of each child or group. You may want to assign different target numbers to different groups, based on children's abilities.

2 Before letting children play, it helps to model how to make a few different number sentences that equal the same target number. You may want to do this on an overhead or on the blackboard.

3 If children lack understanding of the order of operations (i.e. That in a problem like: **8 – 2 x 3**, they must mulitply before subtracting), make sure that if number sentences use multiplication, multiplication precedes addition or subtraction. Example: Children may write a problem like **3 x 4 - 2** (since multiplication precedes subtraction), but not a problem like **12 – 2 x 5** (in which multiplication follows subtraction). And tell children to work all such problems from left to right.

4 If children are familiar with order of operations, they may set up problems like **8 – 2 x 3**, and then you can use this game to test how well they understand the solving procedure.

5 Show children that they can use two cards side by side to represent a two-digit number. Example: 4 to the left and 7 to its right represents 47. Make sure children can create two-digit numbers before they play.

6 If your children think faster without cards than with them, let children abandon cards and just write down number sentences on Target Number Worksheet.

7 After play, hold a class sharing time when children's answers are displayed for all. Promote a discussion to discover patterns in number sentences. e.g. If Target Number is 5, one group might come up with these sentences: **30 – 25 + 0 = 5; 30 – 26 + 1 = 5; 30 – 27 + 2 = 5; 30 – 28 + 3 = 5**, etc. Children might describe such a pattern by saying: "The first number stays the same. But the next two numbers both go up by one."

Horseshoes
Sample Number Sentences Master

Game A Sample: Target Number = 6

Game B or C Sample:
Target Number = 16
Restriction: Use multiplication
and addition once each.

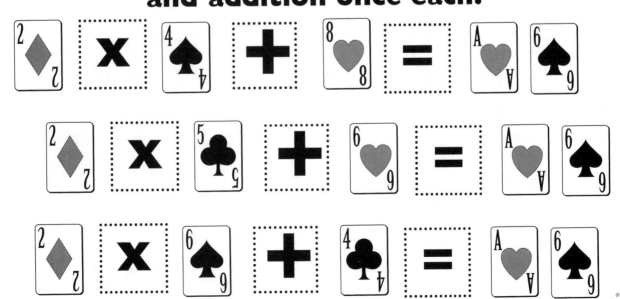

85

Horseshoe Symbol Master

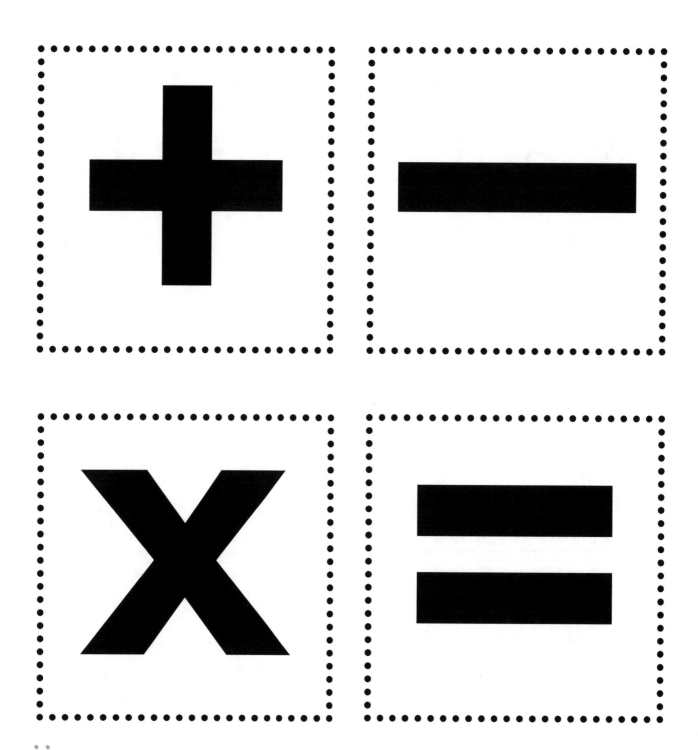

Horseshoe Master

Target Number
Worksheet Master

Children playing: _____, _____, _____, _____

Target Number: _____

_____ = _____

_____ = _____

_____ = _____

Target Number: _____

_____ = _____

_____ = _____

_____ = _____

Target Number: _____

_____ = _____

_____ = _____

_____ = _____

Target Number: _____

_____ = _____

_____ = _____

_____ = _____

Horseshoe Gameboard Master

Children playing: _____, _____, _____, _____

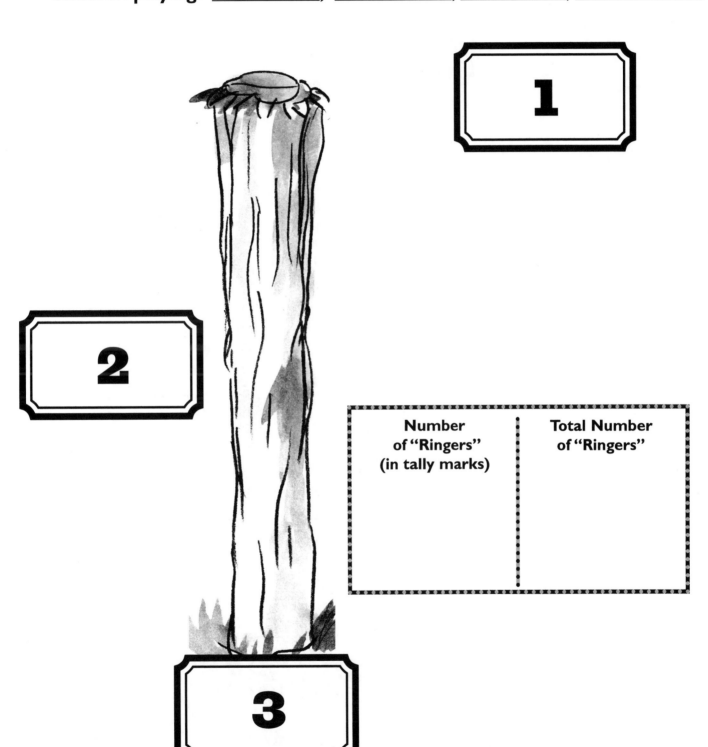

1

2

3

Number of "Ringers" (in tally marks)	Total Number of "Ringers"

STORYLINE

After a busy roundup, young cowhands engage in a competition to test their mental powers. They try to guess if a face-down card is red or black, and they keep track of how many guesses they get right. By looking at their data, they get a taste for the process of elimination, which can help them through many a fix.

CONCEPT CORRAL

DATA ANALYSIS & PROBABILITY
➻ Observe and record data.

➻ Study data to make educated guesses.

REASONING
➻ Learn the process of elimination (POE).

REPRESENTATION
➻ Show whether a guess is right or wrong by recording it correctly on a data chart.

Galloping Guesses

GAME A Cooperative

GOAL: To make as many correct guesses as possible about whether a face-down card is red or black.

 # Players: 1, 2, 3, or 4.

1 Deck of 20 cards is shuffled and placed on table face down. One child begins by guessing if top card is black or red. After guessing, this child turns top card over where all can see it.

2 Child to right of first child records whether guess was right or wrong by making a mark on Galloping Guesses Data Sheet, copied off master on p.92. Child first locates space corresponding to card turned over. Example: If card is 6 of diamonds, find space for 6 of ♦. If card is 6 of spades, find space for the 6 of ♠. If guess is right, child adds a smile to face; if guess is wrong, child adds a frown to face.

3 Children take turns guessing, then turning over one card at a time until all 20 cards have been played. Children can help each other make good guesses by using the process of elimination (POE). See Campfire Chat #2.

4 Once all 20 cards are turned over, children count number of correct guesses and write it on line at bottom of Data Sheet.

GAME B Competitive

GOAL: To make the most correct guesses about whether the cards are red or black.

 # Players: 2, or 4. With 4, you may want to play pair vs. pair.

Same rules as in Game A, only now each child or pair of children tries to make more correct guesses than her opponent(s).

1 How many correct guesses would you make if you guessed either black or red for all 20 cards? **A: You would get exactly 10 correct guesses, since there are exactly 10 black cards and 10 red cards.**

***2** Can it help you to think about the information on your worksheet before you guess? How can this help you make a better guess? **A: Yes. By looking at the info, you can make a better guess. Example: If Data Sheet shows that there are five cards left, and that four of them are black, it makes more sense to guess black than red, for it's more likely that next card is black.**

***3** Can you think of any situations in everyday life when you need to use process of elimination (POE)? **A: Answers will vary, but discussion will elicit ideas.**

4 If someone played this game 100 times, is it likely that he would ever guess all 20 cards correctly? What if someone played it 1,000 times? Why or why not? **A: Answers will vary. But here's an interesting fact. If you flip a coin 20 times in a row, odds of guessing heads or tails correctly all 20 times is about 1 in a million ($1:2^{20}$). That's a situation involving just luck (no data analysis or process of elimination). It's impossible to calculate the odds for Galloping Guesses, however, because the order of the cards varies, and POE allows you to make better guesses as you go.**

FOR EACH PLAYER OR GROUP OF PLAYERS:

➤ All cards from Ace through 10 in one black suit and all cards from Ace through 10 in one red suit. Example: Use all 10 cards from Ace of spades through 10 of spades and all 10 cards from Ace of hearts through 10 of hearts.

➤ Game A: One copy per group of Galloping Guesses Data Sheet, copied off master on p.92.

➤ Game B: One copy per child of Galloping Guesses Data Sheet.

TIPS AND POINTERS

1 In individual play, child guesses and records by himself. If 2, 3, or 4 play cooperatively, each child takes a turn guessing and turning over a card while other children record on Data Sheet.

2 Before children play, it helps to model how to record guesses on Data Sheet. Tell children that they first find the space on the Data Sheet corresponding to turned-over card, and only then do they record — with an upturned mouth ("happy face") for a correct guess, or a downturned mouth ("sad face") for an incorrect guess.

3 It helps to "think aloud" as you demonstrate game to bring out its process-of-elimination aspects. Useful questions to ask aloud are:

➤ How many black cards have been played?

➤ Knowing that there are 10 black cards altogether, can we figure out how many blacks are left?

➤ Of the cards that are left, can we figure out how many are black and how many are red?

➤ Can this information help us make a good guess?

4 Educators may remind children to stop and count the number of cards of each color before making guesses.

Galloping Guesses Data Sheet

RED CARDS			BLACK CARDS		
A	♥ or ♦	😮	A	♣ or ♠	😮
2	♥ or ♦	😮	2	♣ or ♠	😮
3	♥ or ♦	😮	3	♣ or ♠	😮
4	♥ or ♦	😮	4	♣ or ♠	😮
5	♥ or ♦	😮	5	♣ or ♠	😮
6	♥ or ♦	😮	6	♣ or ♠	😮
7	♥ or ♦	😮	7	♣ or ♠	😮
8	♥ or ♦	😮	8	♣ or ♠	😮
9	♥ or ♦	😮	9	♣ or ♠	😮
10	♥ or ♦	😮	10	♣ or ♠	😮

Number of correct guesses: _____

How to Make a Simple, Effective Card Holder

Method A — (Easier, but less secure)

MATERIALS NEEDED:

➤ Two lids from cottage cheese, sour cream, or butter tubs.

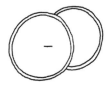

➤ One brad.

DIRECTIONS:

1. Poke a hole with a long-arm hole puncher or a sharp scissor in the center of each lid.

2. Place the covers back to back, so they are directly against each other and connect with the brad.

TO USE: Have children stick the cards between the two lids and hold onto the lids with their hands.

• •

Method B — (Bit harder, but more secure)

MATERIALS NEEDED:

➤ Two lids from cottage cheese, sour cream, or butter tubs.

➤ Two buttons.

➤ One piece of pipe cleaner.

DIRECTIONS:

1. Make two small holes in the center of each lid.
2. Place the covers back to back, so they are directly against each other.
3. Place a 1/2"-3/4" button over the two holes, one on each side.
4. Use the pipe cleaner to connect the buttons and lids together.
5. Twist the pipe cleaner and cut off the extra.

TO USE: Have children stick the cards between the two lids and hold onto the lids with their hands.

Side view ➡

Notes

Notes

NCTM Standards Inventory

GAME	PAGES	Number & Operation	Algebra & Patterns	Geometry	Measurement	Data & Probability	Problem Solving	Reasoning & Proof	Communication	Connections	Representation
"Nine-Second" Ned	6–9	✓				✓					
Annie Oakley	10–15					✓		✓	✓	✓	✓
Hunting for Grub	16–21	✓	✓		✓			✓	✓	✓	
Roundup Rivals	22–27	✓				✓		✓	✓		
Steer on the Loose!	28–33	✓	✓				✓		✓	✓	
Sizing up Snakes	34–37				✓			✓	✓	✓	✓
Battle for Cattle	38–41	✓	✓						✓		
Quicksand	42–45	✓	✓						✓		✓
The Bum Steer	46–49		✓				✓	✓	✓		
Land Grab	50–53		✓				✓	✓	✓		
"High Five!"	54–59	✓				✓		✓	✓		
Bucking Bronco	60–65	✓	✓			✓		✓	✓		
Fix the Fence	66–69	✓	✓				✓	✓	✓		
Mysterious Bandits	70–75	✓	✓				✓	✓	✓	✓	
Cows in the Pen	76–81	✓		✓						✓	
Horseshoes	82–89	✓						✓		✓	
Galloping Guesses	90–92					✓		✓	✓		✓